GOLDEN WIZDOM
BEYOND THE EMERALD CITY

A Conscious Journey to Wholeness

Ilene Kimsey
in association with the
Century-Old Masters of Oz

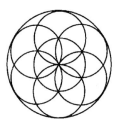

Toto-ly Ozsome Publishing
Loveland, Colorado

Library of Congress Card Catalog Number: 00-191432
ISBN 0-9700477-0-3

Edited by Shirley Parrish
Book layout and design by Ilene Kimsey and Dee Koury
Book printed by Citizen Printing Company, Fort Collins, CO

This book may be purchased from your local bookstore or directly from the publisher.

Toto-ly Ozsome Publishing
P. O. Box 96
Loveland, Colorado 80539

This book is dedicated to the memory of my parents, Helen Farrell Kimsey and J. Lyle Kimsey, whose powerful love and respect for one another continues to reverberate in my soul. Their spirit of joy, belief in the good of humanity, and practical application of love have guided my journey.

CONTENTS

ACKNOWLEDGMENTS

I am deeply grateful to L. Frank Baum, who opened himself to the pure inspiration that guided him to write, *The Wonderful Wizard of Oz*. The journey he set in motion touched my heart and continues to evolve within my life.

A special thank you to Marshall Stewart Ball, author of *Kiss of God*. His ability to paint great masterpieces with a few words encouraged me to honor the power of every word.

Appreciation overflows to Mary Shada for her ever present insights, to Carol Makana Berg for years of multi dimensional support as this project grew from infancy to maturity, and to Anne Smigelsky, for reflecting the bounty and benevolence of the Universe.

Thank you to my editor, Shirley Parrish, whose ability to integrate logic and love created a delightful working relationship. In addition, special recognition to Tina Kingery, Colleen Schreiner, Lani Yamasaki, Tom Aron and Lynn Roberts for their editing wisdom. My heartfelt appreciation to Katie Carroll for our many hours of talking walks. A special acknowledgement to Melissa Ireland, Matthew Hutchison, Tom Pfeffer, Stephanie Staebell, Aina Badua, Wally Amos, Susie Quick, Krystle Brandt, Pollyann Baird and Robert Kory. Each of you have been a unique gift in my life.

Thanks, as well, to Dan Mapes, whose very being celebrates the power of love and the wisdom of the soul. I am profoundly grateful for the heights you have helped me reach that were impossible to reach alone.

I acknowledge No'eau, who gracefully weaves energy into a dance of color. Your artistic mastery has brought this book to life. Thank you for the delight of co-creating this gift of love.

To the Circles of Light group for the opportunity to experience the practical application and loving power of being One out of many.

My gratitude to my brothers and sisters for the lifetime of delightful memories we created. As Daddy-Lyle used to say, "I'd like you to meet our *very unusual children,* the Kimsey Kids, Dianne, Bob, Ilene, Alan, Barbara, Gwen, and Annette."

To all who are on this journey to wholeness, I am deeply honored to share a part of life's adventure with you. There is so very much for us celebrate.

FOREWORD

My great grandfather, L. Frank Baum, wrote the Oz books, and others, for the young-in-heart, to entertain and to "gladden the heart." The lasting messages of Love, Heart, Courage and Wisdom are nestled within his imagination and dreams.

Ilene Kimsey offers us her own wonderful wisdom, inspired by *The Wonderful Wizard of Oz*, to guide us toward our very best in life. Her approach is dynamically insightful and simple; herein lies her genius. This "Conscious Journey to Wholeness" helps us to connect with our inner selves.

Let's hold hands with Ilene and journey beyond the Emerald City. I believe you will find it an *OZsome* adventure. I did.

Roger S. Baum
Author and great grandson of L. Frank Baum

INTRODUCTION

Congratulations! Choosing this book indicates you are a traveler on your way into the vast wisdom of your spirit, the expansion of your mind, the power of your heart, and the knowledge of your body. Like many of us on the road of life, you have probably seen signs along the way. The most well-known billboards are those with the questions asked by us, *Who am I? Why am I here? Where am I going? What am I looking for?*

The purpose of *Golden Wizdom Beyond The Emerald City* is to bring illumination to these divine inquiries and to support one another in remembering the answers. Life is a journey that gives us the adventurous opportunity to explore our unique responses to these questions.

You join the ranks of Greek philosophers, noted psychologists, famous artists, and spiritual leaders who have pondered life's meaning. *The Wizard of Oz* characters are another group of masters who have actively pursued these questions. These well-known travelers have remarkable expertise in finding their way and seeking their heart's desire.

With over 100 years of experience, the mature and evolved characters of *The Wizard of Oz* are ready to mentor you in remembering your unique wisdom. Your personal mastery is yours for the asking. There is a council of authority that lies within you. These advisors will present simple transformational tools to activate your inherent mastery.

Life is a journey to wholeness. "Great!" you might reply, "but how do I get there?" You have already taken your first step into this most unusual opportunity of self-discovery. Through the guidance of these eight personal consultants, you have specialized expertise at your service. The wisdom gained on the journey to Oz will be presented to you as a resource to explore your life's journey. The Oz Masters will present you with fifty *Golden Touchstones* and eight *Golden Wizdom Guidelines* that can change your life.

As with any trip, it is good to be awake so you can consciously experience where you have chosen to go. This Golden Wizdom journey will assist you in waking up to who you truly are. By the time you finish this book you will have ventured into the physical, mental, emotional, and spiritual realms of your radiant self. You will experience the power of achieving your heart's desire through whole being integration. You will engage in a loving and powerful relationship with yourself and have fun remembering your *oz*some wholeness. This is your journey home to your magnificence. The century-old Masters of Oz will be your personal tour guides to exploring your life through the wisdom of your heart.

I first met the Oz characters through the words of L. Frank Baum in his 1900 American Classic, *The Wonderful Wizard of Oz*. I became intrigued with their adventures during my childhood. Our Kansas family gathered annually around the television, and thanks to the magnificent MGM production, traveled the Yellow Brick Road with the Oz characters to the Emerald City.

Since my Mother's death in 1983, I have been in a very personal relationship with *The Wizard of Oz* characters. While deep in the grieving process and questioning the meaning of life, insights from the characters began to come to me. These messages of wisdom and comfort guided me through this deep loss.

One day during my daily run, I experienced an overwhelming pain in my heart. The ache filled the void of Mother's loving presence. Tears flooded down my face. In that moment, I remembered a scene from *The Wizard of Oz* film. The image was that of Dorothy running home very distraught because Miss Gulch was going to take her dog, Toto, and have him destroyed. I heard Aunt Em's response to Dorothy's concern, "Now Dorothy dear—stop imagining things . . . you always get yourself into a fret over nothing."

Mother had been the unconditional love to me that Dorothy experienced with Toto. My whole life turned upside down, and it felt as if society were saying to me, "Now Ilene dear—stop imagining things . . . you always get yourself into a fret over nothing."

A wave of memories swept over me. There were so many times when I had not honored the reality of my imaginings, of my feelings, of my knowing. Instead, I had opted to trust what was truth for others. On that day, I swore to myself that I would never dishonor what I knew as real. I claimed my belief, like Dorothy, that somewhere over the rainbow the dreams that you dare to dream really do come true.

One day, some months later, it seemed as if all the characters joined in one voice saying,

Ilene, we are nearly 100 years old. We have made the journey to the Emerald City and know all we were searching for lies within. Each of us is a Master in our own right, as are you. We are ready to be seen as who we really are, not who we were. We are no longer

searching. We know. It is time for people to embrace their knowing and mastery. Will you assist us?

I responded with a resounding, "Yes!" From that point forward, I saw Dorothy's experience of traveling the Yellow Brick Road to the Emerald City as a metaphor for my journey. For the next five years, I investigated every aspect of myself through the persona of each Oz character. I embraced the story as a map for my life and discovered that a whole new world exists *beyond* the Emerald City.

In my continuing evolution, I realize the journey to the Emerald City is the journey to the heart. The heart is a sacred portal where Spirit and matter unite. This portal of love is a gateway to total integrity with your body, mind, and spirit at a new level of consciousness. Living in this state of awareness is living in the power of your personal authority. When intentions are clear, you can create life from a place of true power—the power of love.

In my thirty years as a human development professional, I have worked with many people, searching for answers to the meaning of life. Through my relationship with the story and characters of *The Wizard of Oz,* I have recognized the profound knowledge of self-transformation available through this American classic. For that reason, I have chosen to use the Oz metaphor and the adventures of the evolved Oz Masters to explore inner wisdom.

These century-old Masters of Oz are profound guides. Their wisdom is the gold that lies, not at the end of the rainbow, but at its very center. My purpose in writing *Golden Wizdom Beyond The Emerald City* is to introduce you to the Oz characters in their mastery.

These centurions have integrated the wisdom gained from their adventures in the Land of Oz and beyond. They now pass the legacy of Golden Wizdom on to you. Welcome to this experience of life through *emerald eyes*, the eyes of love.

THE JOURNEY

INVITATION FROM THE MASTERS OF OZ

Dear Fellow Traveler,

Greetings from the Land of Oz, the place within where true love lies. In Oz your thoughts create the moment, your heart's desire is realized, and your royalty is recognized.

We are Dorothy, Toto, the Scarecrow, Tin Woodman, and the Lion. You may recognize us as the characters from The Wizard of Oz. *Our friends, the Witch of the North, Witch of the West, and the Wizard are joining us for this ozsome venture of* Golden Wizdom Beyond The Emerald City.

We came into being in 1900 through the magnificent creativity of L. Frank Baum and his book, The Wonderful Wizard of Oz. *In 1939, MGM added other dimensions to our lives in the film by the same title. We continue to expand our awareness of who we are as we integrate all that we have learned on the journey.*

In the early years we yearned for something more:
If I only had a brain.
If I only had a heart.
If I only had courage.
If I could only get back home.

We are no longer searching for home, longing for a brain, a heart, or courage. We have discovered that all that we were looking for lies within each of us. There is so

19

much that has happened in our lives since we traveled down the Yellow Brick Road to the Emerald City.

Just as you have grown in your conscious awareness over the years, we have also evolved. We now know that each of us is a Master and that all of us are truly Toto-ly Ozsome. We look forward to continuing our journey beyond the Emerald City and invite you to join us.

We greet you today recognizing your wisdom. Whether you are five, thirty-five or ninety-five, we know that you know that you are totally awesome. If in this moment, you have forgotten that truth, we are here to help you remember.

This journey with us will take you back to the wholeness of yourself. You will be reawakened to the wisdom of your mind, the wisdom of your heart, the wisdom of your body, and the wisdom of your spirit. You will remember how to honor the vastness of who you are.

You are cordially invited to join us:

This is a REUNION of all that has gone on before with all that is yet to come.

This is an INVITATION to wake up to the knowing that all you are searching for lies within.

This is an ANNOUNCEMENT that this life you live is a journey back home to yourself.

This is a DECLARATION that who you really are is Love in form.

This is a MESSAGE from beyond the Rainbow to your soul to remind you of your many dimensions.

This is a REQUEST for your conscious participation in your life.

This is a KNOWING that you are a part of each of us and we are a part of you.

It is our pleasure to share with you the Golden Wizdom we have learned along the Yellow Brick Road to the Emerald City and beyond.

As we journey, so do you.
As you journey, so do we.

Our experience, awareness and insights about life are offered in this book. May you find yourself among the pages.

With the Golden Wizdom of Love, we are,

Dorothy,
Toto,
Scarecrow,
Tin Woodman,
Lion,
Witch of Celebration (formerly the Good Witch)
Witch of Transformation (formerly the Wicked Witch)
Wizard

LIVE KNOWING HOME LIES WITHIN

DOROTHY

*I am the wisdom of light that lies
within the innocence of you.*

Reflections on Living Life Fully

I am Dorothy. I know that home lies within. My journey to this awareness began long before the turbulent twister swept me into the flight of my life.

L. Frank Baum ignited my essence within his heart over a century ago. With a stroke of his pen, I found myself on a drought-ridden Kansas farm with Aunt Em, Uncle Henry, and my beloved dog, Toto. Even though life appeared gray, I held the promise of the rainbow in my heart.

One day a Kansas storm ushered in a spiraling energy that carried me beyond myself to the wonders of the Land of Oz. Toto and I were surrounded with extraordinary friends and marvelous adventures in this place of new perspectives.

My association with the Scarecrow, Tin Woodman, and the Lion demonstrated the power of working together as One. We each had a unique and powerful determination to find our heart's desire. It was that common purpose that moved us forward along the Yellow Brick Road to the Emerald City. What we discovered independently was astounding, and what we accomplished together was profound.

My journey through Oz gave me a new foundation of reality and expanded my inner knowing. I delight in sharing with you some of my *oz*some discoveries for living life to its fullest. Come, let us journey home together.

Beyond the Rainbow

As a child, I remember the longing deep inside me to see more, to be more, and to know more about life. I felt a tremendous desire to walk across the bridge of the rainbow to discover what was on the other side. There was a core part of me that knew what was beyond, but I could not quite remember. At times, this veiled inner knowing was more real for me than my life on the farm.

Life in Kansas was sometimes gray. It was not because we had no sunshine, our existence was simply without passion. We moved through each day accomplishing tasks, however, the joy and wonderment that lived in my soul was rarely expressed.

Sometimes I would see a flicker of delight in Aunt Em's eyes, as if there were a time when she knew true joy. Uncle Henry had an abundance of humor within him, but he locked it up like a secret of the past. I experienced their love, even though their caring came in tight packages of concern and worry.

It seemed to agitate Aunt Em when I would share my dreams with her. She'd always say, "You're wasting your time child. Get your head out of the clouds and your feet back on the ground. Disappointment is all you'll get from dreaming."

Worry appeared to be what Aunt Em knew best. She seemed to believe that if she prepared for the worst, she would not know disappointment. Enough fretting could avoid a disaster. Aunt Em was confident that the more she worried about me, the more she was expressing her love. Although I came to accept this way of loving, there was a void where delight belonged.

Sometimes I wondered if Aunt Em believed that happiness could not exist in the same space as life. There were moments when I saw joy unexpectedly creep in and laughter rise out of her like the Old Faithful geyser. Those times were rare, but I savored them like a rainy day during a drought.

Aunt Em and Uncle Henry were good people. They loved me dearly and raised me in a manner that made sense to them. When times were lonely, I would tell my dog, Toto, of my heart's desire to travel beyond the rainbow. He listened. He seemed to understand. His unconditional love helped me keep the dreams alive.

Before I came to live with Aunt Em and Uncle Henry, I knew there was a place where joy and adventure thrived. I knew there were astonishing things beyond my thoughts and visions. This knowing lived in my soul with Technicolor reality and no amount of gray would ever take it away.

The Promise

Before the drought dried up most of Uncle Henry's hope, he revealed his wisdom of the rainbow. "It's the promise," he said. "The promise between Heaven and Earth."

I remember the day we sat on the fence near the wheat field. The glistening moisture had blessed the golden crop. As the rainbow began to grace the sky, Uncle Henry said, "There's both science and magic to the rainbow. The rainbow is formed opposite of the sun by the refraction and reflection of the sun's rays in the rain. The magic is that the rainbow is as vast as your imagination."

As we watched the arc of color in silence, I saw life radiate for the first time on Uncle Henry's face. As he looked at me and smiled, it was as if he passed a heritage of rainbow gifts to me for safekeeping. We never spoke of our quiet miracle, yet it lives as my strongest memory of Uncle Henry. He returned to the haven of his work, and I tucked my rainbow gifts away in my heart.

For the next two years, the heavens held the rain captive. The parched land begged for moisture with only more dehydration as a response. It seemed the rainbow had become a fantasy.

I would often return to the wheat field fence, calling forth the memory of the rainbow from my heart. I would bask in its refreshing color and feel the life of the promise. It was this dive into the waters of my imagination that brought the wellspring of rainbow gifts to light. One by one I unwrapped each precious gem to find the wisdom of the rainbow:

There is a relationship between light and delight.

Each color stands next to the other in full spectrum harmony.

Life is simple, yet profound.

Rainbows reflect our many dimensions.

That which cannot be touched can be real.

The bridge of light that reaches beyond also reaches within.

The promise between Heaven and Earth awakens in the heart.

Each day I weave the wisdom of the rainbow into the tapestry of my soul. I will forever unwrap its magic, for the rainbow is as vast as my imagination.

The Tornado Brings a New Perspective

I have heard the deafening silence. I have been enveloped in the pressured stillness of the moments before the great whirlwind. The spiraling power of a tornado can strike as fast as lightning and leave chaos and disaster in its wake.

Growing up in Kansas, I knew the importance of respecting tornadoes. The first thing I learned was to get out of their way. The second was to prepare for the potential aftermath. Aunt Em, Uncle Henry, Toto, and I would go to the cellar with our stored provisions of candles, water, and canned food. In that refuge the twister could not penetrate the sanctuary of the earth.

One summer day the wind wailed out of the north. "There's a twister coming," Uncle Henry call to Aunt Em, "I'll go look after the stock." Then he ran to the barn to tend to the cows and horses.

"Quick, Dorothy," Aunt Em screamed, "Run for the cellar." Frightened, she threw open the cellar door and climbed down the stairs to the dark safety.

Before I could get to the cellar, the shrieking wind shook the house and I fell. The swirling winds carried the house, Toto, and me, into a spiraling ascent. In a surprisingly gently fashion, the tornado set the house down in a place distinctively different from Kansas. This instant change of perspective altered my life forever. My world shifted and I saw life from an expanded point of view.

Although few people have experienced a Kansas tornado, most have known some type of turmoil in their life. The devastation of a personal tragedy can rip through our emotional, mental, or spiritual life just as a tornado tears through our home. The death of a loved one, break-up of a relationship, illness, or the loss of a dream can cause us to feel swallowed up and spit out into a hundred pieces.

The great dichotomous wisdom of the tornado is that peace lies in the midst of chaos.

When I attempt to control a tumultuous situation, I can become caught up in the debris and lose my focus. I realize that I cannot control the chaos, nor can I pull someone from the turmoil to the center. We must all find the calm within ourselves. When I live from the still point within, I flow with the changes and spiral to a new awareness.

Small, Yet Mighty

The wisdom of children is sometimes overlooked because of their small stature. As a child, I often felt that what I knew within me was larger than common words could express. Sharing an insightful observation with Aunt Em usually lost something in the translation. My images of grandeur were often dismissed as childish fantasy.

The Land of Oz brought to life my visions of splendor and instantly authenticated the reality of my inner world. The tornado spiraled me to the eastern quadrant of Oz, the land of the Munchkins. My house landed on the Witch of the East who held the little people in bondage for many years. They were in awe of my accidental heroism and gave me a generous and kind-hearted welcome. The Munchkins, whose full grown height matched my child size, danced about with joy, freely celebrating their independence.

Being in the presence of so many little people empowered my sense of sovereignty. There was a vibrancy and grace about them that was contagious. This Munchkin experience ignited my inner creativity and kept the flames of pure wisdom burning throughout my childhood.

The little people continue to have a very significant place in my heart. Though my time with them was brief, its meaning was vast. The Munchkins inspired an awareness to notice the immensity that can be present in something small.

Power of the heart - Strength of the spirit
Expanse of the mind - Wisdom of the body
Small phrases with mighty messages.

Sole / Soul Purpose

Since my early childhood I have felt an inner awareness that my sole purpose was to discover an important truth. This call to exploration sang out from the depths of me. I knew that if I followed this beckoning to truth, one day I would remember my soul purpose.

My childhood sense of adventure did not fit with the practical matters Aunt Em wanted me to accomplish. She experienced my life as perplexing and encouraged me to find a place where I would stay out of trouble. Little did she know that her directive triggered my imagination and took me even farther away from her daily reality.

I wondered if there were a place behind the moon or beyond the rain where there wasn't any trouble. My curiosity became realized the day the twister carried Toto and me to the unexplored territory of Oz. The magnificent splendor was far beyond my wildest imaginings. We were definitely not in Kansas anymore. Much to my surprise, I longed for home immediately. All that I saw and experienced intrigued me. Yet, my single focus was to return to that which was familiar.

In the Land of Munchkins, a wise and magical woman explained that perhaps the Wizard of Oz could help me find my way back home. She said I would have to walk to the Emerald City which was at the center of the country. She gave me the shoes of the Witch of the East for my journey. The Witch no longer needed them, for my house had landed on her. The wise woman said there was some charm connected with the shoes.

At first, my only concern was that the shoes fit comfortably for the many miles I had to travel. Upon placing them on my feet, I experienced a feeling of friendly support. With each step, the sole embraced the hallowed ground. As I continued my journey to find my way back home, the shoes guided me on a path of much adventure and provided a new understanding of myself.

I learned that the shoes had the power to carry me to any place I chose. All I needed to do was to click the heels together three times. Although I am not sure I fully understood it, I knew there was power in three. Within the expansion of three, polarity melts away. The wholeness of three embraces body, mind, and spirit. "Go" is what happens after "One, Two, Three." I clicked my heels together three times. In the wink of an eye I was back home.

To this very day, I continue to click my heels together three times. I am carried to wonderful places and always feel at home. I have come to understand that the reason for my journey to Oz was to discover my soul's purpose: To live life with the awareness that home lies within.

Surrender—A Short Cut Home

"Surrender, Dorothy," the Witch of the West wrote across the sky for all to see. Even though frightened, there was no way I was going to surrender to her or anyone. Giving up or yielding to her power was not an option. My total focus was on getting to the Wizard so he could help me return home. This determination was my strength.

In later years as I reflected on the experience, I realized that which I feared, the Witch, had brought me a valuable message. Surrender has many different levels of meaning. Some people experience surrender as "giving up." For me, it is the process of "opening up" to receive all that I am.

As I surrender my doubts and fears, I clear the path to experience more of my magnificence. Releasing the thoughts, beliefs, and attitudes that hold me in bondage allows space for my spirit to freely expand. Indeed, surrendering is my short cut home to the fullness of me.

The Rest of the Journey

On our journey to the Emerald City, we came upon a meadow carpeted with a plethora of beautiful flowers. As we went deep into the poppy field, I became very drowsy. The scent was so powerful that it lulled me to sleep. Not being of flesh and bone, the Scarecrow and Tin Woodman were unaffected by the potent aroma. They guided me out of the sleep-inducing field. As I lay at the meadow's edge, a fresh breeze danced around my body and awakened me to conscious awareness.

I am grateful that my friends supported me in returning to the Yellow Brick Road. Although somewhat disconcerting, my slumber in the flowers had been refreshing. We reoriented ourselves and continued the rest of the journey to the Emerald City and beyond.

Since that time, I have reflected on my experience in the field of poppies. Rest is important on a journey of any kind. Taking a break can support rejuvenation and be an opportunity for reassessing commitment to your destination. The choice to fall asleep or enter a subconscious state can benefit the journey. On the whole, a key is to keep focused on where you intend to go.

Grand ideas have ascended from my creative subconscious. Explorations in my sleep have brought forward hidden revelations to my conscious living. This honoring of the mutual wisdom of conscious and subconscious has opened me to knowing more aspects of myself. With each choice I make, I have the clear intention of consciously experiencing the journey.

Wisdom of Innocence

I used to take innocence for granted. Innocence brings clarity of thought, purity of heart, vision beyond seeing, and the experience of being One with everything. Although innocence is inherent to childhood, it can quickly become lost along the way.

The robbers of innocence come in many forms. The devastation of a drought, despair of a loved one, or the greed of a witch, can each impair belief in a benevolent world. I have seen disrespect slam the door on innocence. I have known fear to swallow the key. It takes courage to reclaim purity of heart, and a sincere willingness to reactivate inner knowing.

My encounters with adversity in Oz were my initiation to a deeper wisdom. When faced with life's paradoxical experiences, I discovered that my core virtues brought clarity. Life's journey is an opportunity to consciously activate another dimension of the wisdom of innocence. The more I embrace the simplicity of impeccable truth, the more profound my life becomes.

Innocence is not ignorant naiveté. Innocence is pure, natural wisdom. Mature innocence is the conscious choice to live in the fullness of my thoughts, my heart, my vision, and my wholeness. I acknowledge the power and wisdom of innocence.

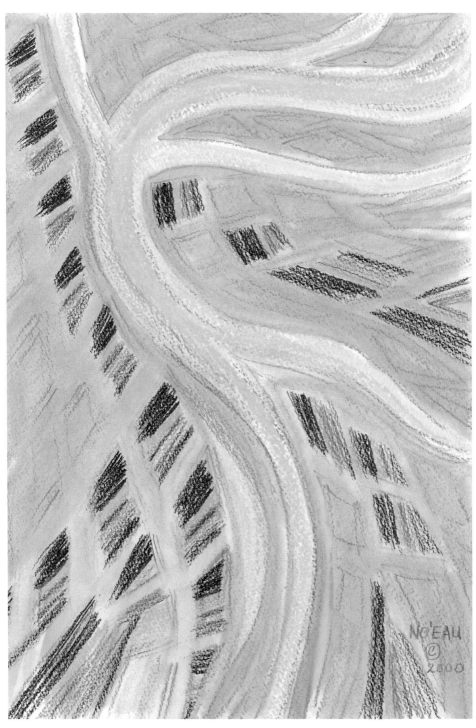

*Each day I weave the wisdom of the rainbow
into the tapestry of my soul.*

Dream Stepping

Am I dreaming my dreams or are my dreams dreaming me? What is real takes on a new meaning when you have been over the rainbow. Before my journey to Oz, my dreams were where I experienced the adventure of life. My imagination was the playground of new possibilities.

Dreams are an open canvas for my limitless creation. Whether I am dreaming in my sleep or accessing my imagination while awake, the uncharted territory is divine. In this space, I hold images that are void of any constraints. I allow thoughts and feelings to take me beyond where I have been before. I delight in stepping into my dreams for they are where everything first emerges.

My dream world has often been the stage for rehearsing coming attractions. It is a place where I dare to dance with my imagination and experience other aspects of myself. The power felt in overcoming adversity and the magic of creating a new moment are gifts of the dream time, waking or asleep.

Emotion is the bridge that brings the land of dreams to the vitality of the day. Dreams become real through emotion. When I latch onto the feelings I experience in my imagination, they serve as a conduit for transforming my dreams into reality. When I allow myself to experience the emotional power of dreams, I open doorways to my soul.

A giant portal opened the day I awakened in the Land of Oz. As I took my first step, my reality expanded. I was a stranger in a strange land, and my eyes embraced each exquisite scene with freshness. The marvelous beauty of the countryside and the vibrant color of the flora took my breath away.

The friends I met, and the adventures I experienced, have become forever etched in my heart. The journey to the Emerald City, which lies at the very center of Oz, was also my journey to a deeper part of myself. The dormant corners of my consciousness became activated as if recovering from a hypnotic trance. Oz brought me to a wholeness I did not realize I had abandoned. The exploration offered me a broader view of reality.

I have invited Oz into my waking hours. I realize that the veil between the dream time and the dreamer is thinning. Imagination is alive and well in each moment, and I am experiencing the grace of my living dream.

The Yellow Brick Road

"Can you help me find my way?" I asked the wise woman.

"Always best to start at the beginning. All you do is follow the Yellow Brick Road. It will lead you to the City of Emeralds."

The spiraling bright yellow path arose from the center of the eastern quadrant of Oz, like the sun rises daily in the eastern sky. Toto and I followed the solar-charged path to the edge of Munchkinland and bid farewell to our newfound friends. The radiant road stretched before us, directing our steps to an unknown destiny.

Being clear about my goal of returning *home* was a very important factor in keeping me on the path. There were so many challenges and opportunities along the way that could have led me in other directions. I met three fellow travelers, committed to accomplishing their heart's desire. Our mutual intent strengthened our individual resolve, and we each gained a higher level of awareness of what we value.

My journey down the Yellow Brick Road brought me home to a golden light that lies within my core. The warm glow of this personal power radiates with each step I take since my adventures in Oz. The Emerald City is a magical place where I recognized that what I was looking for lives within me.

As I continue my life's spiraling journey, I travel beyond the Emerald City on a road of golden wizdom. All that has come in and gone out of my life is now a part of me, and I am living life more fully that I ever knew possible.

LOVE UNCONDITIONALLY

TOTO

*I am the wisdom of unconditional love
that lies within the essence of your being.*

Instinctual Insights

I am Toto, an expression of unconditional love in the form of a dog.

I am Dorothy's best friend and have been by her side from Kansas to Oz and back again.

I live in the purity of the moment.

I love unconditionally.

My life is an expression of simple profoundness.

I am forever loving of who you are.

Be

Be in the moment—that's all there is. The moment is always better when you are in it. It is the only place where life happens. It is this moment that you have been looking for all along. You had trouble recognizing it because you were so focused on sorting through the past or jumping ahead to the future that you missed it.

When you allow the moment to be you, and you the moment, there is no judgment. The moment is filled with real presence. Real presence equals love.

Love comes in many forms. Even feelings such as anger, jealousy, or disappointment can be expressions of love. It is important to love yourself enough to express the truth of your feelings in the moment. Feelings are not good or bad, they simply are. So, let them *be*. When you attach the past or the future to your feelings, they become encumbered.

I know this is a challenging concept for you, because humans often find difficulty being in the present moment. You sit in judgment of yourself in so many ways. That is why we, your pets, are in your life—your dogs, your cats, your gerbils, your horses . . .

We live in the moment. We are not *doing* anything, we are *being* love. We love you, whether you love yourself or not. We are unconditional love, Toto Love.

46

Live Directly

When I want something, I ask for it.
When I am curious, I investigate.
When I am not interested, I am not interested.
When I am ready for love, I let you know.
When I want to be alone, I create a space for me.

When I am hungry, I eat.
When I am tired, I rest.
When I am ready to play, I play.
When I want company, I find a companion.

I can make almost anything interesting.
I naturally set my boundaries.
I listen keenly.
I respond instinctively.
I am loyal, dependable, and trustworthy.
I enjoy life.
I love without conditions.

A Tail / Tale to Tell

My tail says it all. The old saying, "Dogs wear their emotions on their tails," is true. I communicate my joy, surprise, disappointment, and contentment with my tail. It is a spontaneous action that is always expressing.

When you come home, there is no question that I am happy to see you. You give meaning to tail wagging. This freedom of expression is one of the delights of being a dog.

I would love to give you my tail for a couple of days. Then, you could feel the direct connection between the tail and what you are thinking and feeling. Others would know exactly where you stood on issues. People all around you would see your honest attitude. What kind of tale would that tail tell?

Get the Picture

I have come to this moment with some advice. When you want to communicate something to me, get the picture, then hold it. If you choose to put words with the picture, select one or two that are clear and concise such as: "Come. Sit. Heel. Good dog."

You see, I am very intelligent and I do not need long explanations. I think in pictures. Give me a clear picture along with your words.

There may be times when you are challenged to know what I want. I suggest you free your mind and receive my picture. I'll create the image of what I want. Allow yourself to see my picture.

Life is an Attitude

Both people and animals live with a particular attitude. We have a disposition, approach, or perspective about life. I have noticed that a person's attitude shows up in their every word, thought, and action. I believe that play is a great attitude to have about life. When you see life as play, you move lightly, engage in recreation, and have fun.

When was the last time you giggled?
How long has it been since you put your bare feet on
    the fresh grass,
Or let mud squeeze through your toes?
Do you listen to the birds?
Do you make a wish when you see a falling star?
Is there someone's hand you need to hold?
Who is waiting to receive your smile?
What is the word of tenderness you need to hear?

Today, create a moment to listen to your heart, see the beauty of a flower, or thank a friend for support. A playful attitude can wrap around moments that are tense, or slip into tight places to create a feeling of lightheartedness. Try on an attitude of play for one day. I guarantee, you will move through the world lighter than before.

Simplicity is Profound

Be a best friend.
Run and jump freely.
Take naps.
Be clear about your boundaries.
Stay unattached to outcomes.
Fully experience each moment.
Be trustworthy.
Ask for attention when you want it.
Speak when you have something to say.
Be loyal.
Sit close to those you love.

Try a Little Tenderness

Tenderness.
Do you know it?
Have you seen it?
Have you felt it?
Have you given it?
It is a day for tenderness.

A day to remember who you are and honor the precious life within you.

Tenderness begins from the inside and weaves itself around every breath.

Tenderness is feeling the sun gently upon your face, and recognizing that you have been kissed by the Universe.

Tenderness is hearing the music of the birds or the babbling of a brook, and knowing that the song was meant for you.

Tenderness is hearing the still small voice inside of you, and thanking it for the message.

Tenderness is embracing yourself with the laughter of a child, and realizing it is your delight you are hearing.

Tenderness begins and ends with you, and along the way, it touches many others.

Today, try a little tenderness.

Life is an expression of simple profoundness.

Love Without Conditions

I love without conditions.

My love for you is absolute.

I invite you to love yourself with this spirit of totality.

Service to Humanity

I am here to be of service to humanity through you.

I have a deep compassion and love for who you are.

I am devoted to being ever present as a friend, counselor, guardian, playmate, whatever you need me to be.

I am here to be of service to humanity through you.

BE MINDFUL
THAT
THOUGHTS CREATE

SCARECROW

I am the wisdom of creation that lies within the thought of you.

Thoughts From the Field

I am the Scarecrow. I know thoughts create.

One day, the farmer had a thought to create a scarecrow for his field. He took action and that is how I came to be, from the farmer's thought.

Since 1900 when this thought, that is now me, first occurred, I have had thoughts of my own. In the beginning, I hung mindless in the field. I believed that I could not think because I didn't have a brain. During my life I have been reminded that the essence of thought begins in the heart. This relationship between mind and heart is important for balance in my life.

There is a great deal about the power of thought that I learned out in the field. I respectfully create with my thoughts, bring the thought into form with words, and put the words into the world with my actions. To be conscious is a delight. This is a magnificent journey of creation. Sharing with you is an honor.

Discover Your Field and Honor It

There is a belief among scarecrows that the field where you are placed is your sanctuary. All scarecrows know that they are the guardians of their sacred field. There is a feeling of honor about having a field of your own to watch over. We have a deep sense of pride in keeping nature in balance.

It does not matter where your field is, or what is being grown there. The uniqueness of each field is appreciated. Since scarecrows are not able to walk the field, they send their love like ripples on the water. The love flows out to the edges of the land. Similar to sonar, the love bounces off every living thing and returns to the scarecrow. In this way, the field knows the scarecrow and the scarecrow knows the field.

Others may look at our culture and say that we are of no use, for we simply hang aimlessly in the middle of a piece of land. As with many things in life, there is more happening than meets the eye.

The magic of image in the nation of my mind is guided
by pure joy, love, and divine truth.

The Awakening

In my early days, I experienced satisfaction hanging on a pole in my field. There was comfort knowing my role as a scarecrow.

One day when I was just hanging around, enjoying the beauty of the day, I thought, "I wonder what it would be like to dance down that country road?"

The thought took me by surprise because I had been told I had no brains, only straw in my head. So how could I have a thought? I am not sure if this had ever happened to another scarecrow. I knew it was happening to me. I was thinking. I had ideas.

There were synapses activated in me that were previously unrealized. The thoughtful moment caused an awakening of expanded proportions. It frightened me and filled me with excitement at the same time. A life of thinking. What was ahead for me?

Power of Observation

Observation can become an art form. Observation can bring the unfoldment of mysteries before us. Observation can reveal all the wonders of the world, if we are willing to see them.

I have found there is an attitude that suits observation. It is an attitude of receptivity. I accept the gifts that are laid before me.

Being a scarecrow and working the field for years, I have had many opportunities to observe. I have seen eagles dancing on the edge of air currents, sunsets bringing a fiery exclamation to the day, and the patience of a newly transformed butterfly waiting for its wings to dry.

Ants have taught me about the importance of working together. Corn has demonstrated the power of memory in a seed. The wind has brought gifts from far away places. There is much to see and learn right in front of me. Each day, I choose to open myself to the abundance of every moment.

The Pondering Place

I began to ponder. I had never experienced pondering before. This contemplation triggered memories of stories about my Grandpa. The legend says a neighbor boy helped Grandpa off his pole. They danced down the road to a place beyond the sun. I wonder if Grandpa had experienced thoughts similar to mine? Perhaps he could no longer be satisfied to be stuck on a pole. I was curious if the stories were true or simply tales of straw?

My ancestors had taught me that my role in life was to hang in place until I fell apart. It just seemed there was more to living than hanging out in the same field all your life. I am not putting down the profession. I honor those who have been protecting fields for generations. The fact is, once I had a thought of my own, I was different. The way I perceived my life had changed.

Was I going mad, turning against the scarecrow tradition? Would the community ostracize me? Would I live in separation? Could I be in service to my creator in a place different from where I had initially been stuck?

In one moment my whole world had changed, and things I had done in joyful service now felt like the duties of a prisoner. I did not want to be *hung up* in the middle of a field for the rest of my life. I wanted to explore other fields and far-reaching country roads. How could it happen? I wished Grandpa were here to ask for advice.

As if in response to my thought, I heard a voice:

Good morning. Welcome to the Scarecrow Hour. This is a time when new discoveries about old ways of thinking will be presented to you. This is a time when you'll clear your mind in order to hear what's really going on. This is a time of learning that the way it's been for Scarecrows for

64

centuries is not necessarily the way it is for you. The fields that most of your ancestors have hung in are not your fields. You were created to participate in a much bigger field.

The time has come when you need to decide if you want to go through life with a pole up your butt. This is a rite of passage for you, and this one decision can make a big difference to your world. Ponder this carefully, for your final thought on the matter will influence more than you can imagine.

Stunned by what I heard, I almost fell off my pole. I began to ask a question, but the voice was gone as quickly as it had come. Pondering was indeed a powerful experience. I spent the rest of my day sorting through all the thoughts that had taken place.

Reality is a State of Mind

All of my life I heard others say my head was filled with straw and I could not think. This assumption was part of the scarecrow's belief system. I did not dispute this truth for other scarecrows. I simply discovered my reality was different from theirs.

The day I reached beyond the boundaries of the field with a thought was the day I responded to a call from within to listen. I went *into it* and experienced my first lesson in how to *intuit*. This phenomenon of thought was far beyond any reality I had previously known. I honor my heritage, yet I knew in that moment that I no longer wanted to scare crows for a living.

As the sun rose this morning, I realized it was time for my independence. I have been looking at life through the eyes of others, believing their logic. It is time to uncover all that is true for me. I choose to move forward with my life. What a concept, to move forward. What would that feel like? I know that my next action is to ask for help, for I cannot take this step on my own. Because of my position on this pole, I need help to get down.

I will not let the fact that my head is filled with straw cause me to believe I cannot make choices about my life. Therefore, in this moment, I declare my intention to be as free as the birds that fly around me every day. Instead of staying in this field and falling apart, I choose to stay whole and experience life differently. Reality is a state of mind, and mine has truly expanded.

There is Help Along the Way

As I look around my world today, I see things differently. I realize that even though I am in the same location I have been in all my life, somehow I have moved forward. It appears everything is on its way somewhere. People walk down the country road. Rabbits hop from field to field, eating greens. Seeds break through the ground and reach for the sky. I know I am on the way to where I am going.

The country road brought a little girl and her dog in need of direction. I began speaking with her as she was deciding which way to go. Before I knew it, I requested she remove me from the pole so that I could join her on her journey. She obliged graciously.

With my first step onto the earth, a jolt of energy shot through my feet and into my body like lightning. My life, before that point, had been groundless. I had experienced every inch of my field with my heart, watched over it with my eyes, and knew all the sounds and smells. I had never touched it.

This connection with the earth was more powerful than words can express. With that one step, I made a leap of profound joy into a whole new world.

Falling Apart Can Be a Good Thing

I have had crows carry away parts of me, animals rip off a leg and strong winds blow my insides into the next county. Being flexible is an important aspect of a scarecrow's well-being.

The first time I lost my stuffing, I panicked. I remember crying out, "I'm falling apart! I'm losing myself!" The experience of being dis-membered can be frightening. I was still working in the field then, and the farmer would replace my stuffing or re-create a new appendage for me.

Now that I am out on my own, I have learned to reassemble myself. Sometimes I reclaim a missing piece in its totality. Other times I choose to keep parts and recreate the rest anew.

My form is ever changing. As I continue to re-member myself, I become a grander me. Indeed, falling apart can be a good thing. It is an opportunity to look at all the parts in a new way and make a conscious choice about how to re-create the whole.

Your Thoughts Become You

I lived my life in a certain *state of mind*, even though the farmer gave me no brain. My pole perspective limited my view of what was real, but my carefree spirit expanded my outlook on life.

Travelers would stop by my field and engage in conversation. I learned a great deal about other worlds from them. When they would ask me questions, I would frequently say, "I don't know." I was frustrated and often confused about what was real for me. Once I knew what I didn't want, I realized that I knew something—I knew what I did not want. It was grand, *to know*.

When my feet were on the ground and I was moving forward, the world became my university. The journey to the Emerald City was a dynamic education. The challenges my companions and I faced together provided opportunities for clear thinking. Our dedication to one another was fertile soil for personal growth.

The Wizard helped me open my mind even more for sharper thinking. He also honored the knowledge I already had. There is much that I now re-cognize, *know again* in a new way. I know that the brain transforms thought into action, and that intelligence lies in every cell. I know that changing perspective can change thought, and changing thought can change perspective. I know that the power to think for myself lies in me.

I consciously hold the highest thought form in all I do. My thoughts become me. Are your thoughts becoming to you?

Imagination Inspires

There are worlds beyond my eyes that I have touched with my imagination. The gateway to these splendid places lies in my illuminated mind. In this place of creative thinking, all things are possible. Ideas know no boundaries.

This space of mental magic lives in every one of us. It is here that I can enter the depths of a question and see the answer clearly. This inward sight contains pure accuracy. The images of my deeper consciousness arise to inform me of new options.

My imagination is like the creative research lab of my mind. When I link my feelings with the images of my inner world, the thought moves into physical form with exceptional impact. The magic of image in the nation of my mind is guided by pure love, joy and divine truth.

TRUST YOUR HEART

TIN WOODMAN

*I am the wisdom of truth
that lies within the heart of you.*

Tales of the Heart

I am the Tin Woodman. I trust my heart.

As a Woodman who was once flesh and bone, I know the importance of experiencing the heart in *all matter*. There is a life force that pulsates through my body, mind, emotions, and spirit. It is the active expression of my soul. I see this flow of life's purpose in all existence.

There was a time when I had desensitized myself to feeling life. It was too painful. I disengaged from my heart and for a year stood paralyzed with emptiness. I could not move nor barely speak. My tin had rusted, leaving me virtually non-functional.

Much to my good fortune, two travelers and a dog passed my way one day. I felt a longing to connect and allowed a sound to rise within me. "Oil can," I struggled to exclaim. Oil is essential to keeping me fluid. I needed assistance in lubricating the parts of me that had become immobile.

The response of Dorothy and the Scarecrow to my call was my first step on the road to finding a heart. I joined them on their journey to see the Wizard. My quest for a heart was filled with adventure. It is my delight to share some of what I learned about wholehearted living.

Loss of Self

I was born the son of a Woodman. Like most boys, I took on my father's trade and followed his lead by putting everything I had into my work. I became a skilled craftsman and was recognized as successful and prominent in the community.

After my father died, I took care of my mother as long as she lived. I met a young maiden and came to love her with all my heart. I requested that she marry me and she promised me her hand once I made a home for us.

When we met, she was in the service of a mean old woman who treated her like a slave. I set out to build her a home and have it be the dowry for her hand. Every day I went to the forest to chop wood for our new dwelling. I hardly slept, ate, or even spent time with her. My focus was on building our home. Nothing else mattered.

One day while chopping wood, my ax slipped and cut off my leg. I went to the Tinsmith and had him make me a new leg out of tin. Every time I went to chop wood for our home, the ax slipped and cut off another part of me. I nearly lost my whole self as I became a man with flesh of tin.

I learned that the old woman had arranged with the Witch of the West to put a hex on my ax. She wanted to destroy me so she could keep the young maiden I loved with her. In the process of total concentration on my work, I had sacrificed my body and lost my heart. In the end, I had no feeling for anything or anyone. This devastation caused me to steel myself from the world.

From Ax to Grind to Acts of Kind

My ax was to be my tool to gain the maiden's hand. Instead, it became the source of my separation from myself and in turn, my separation from her.

I blamed the old woman. After all, it was her jealousy that drove her to have a hex placed on my ax. I was angry for how she had victimized me. I had never before known such vexation. It took a great deal of discipline not to raise my ax in rage and destroy all in sight. For years, resentment became my reward for being a victim. I held onto the grudge like a well-earned trophy.

I stuffed the pain of my sadness, anger, and resentment into the depths of my being. In time, this choice disabled my ability to move. In my animosity, I had become my own perpetrator. For a year, I stood in the anguish of my choice, holding the ax upright as a reminder of what judgment and blame can create.

In my stillness, I had plenty of time to realize that I no longer had an *ax to grind* with the old woman or myself. I had a deep desire to lay my burden down, to free past resentments so I could move on with my life.

One day, my desire expressed itself as a young girl, her little dog, and a Scarecrow who stopped to help me. Their act of kindness freed me from my prison of repression. As I began to move my body, I experienced life moving through me again. There was a tremendous relief when I could lay down my ax. I vowed from that day forward that I would only use my ax for acts of kindness.

Body Talk

"I want this pain to stop!" I cried out one day.

Much to my surprise, my body responded, "Well, I finally got your attention. Do you know that I have been calling to you in many ways over the years? You wouldn't listen. In fact, you pretended not to hear. For years you have denied your feelings. You have discounted the connection between your mind, body, and spirit.

"Hey, it's a package deal! This is a partnership and we're either all working together or not. You've been working against the harmony of your whole self for a long time. It seems you needed to push yourself and me to a point of disease before you would pay attention.

"The road back to harmony within me, your body, is to listen and respond each step of the way. Feelings are the avenue of communication. When your back hurts, it's calling out. Ask what it needs and how you can support it.

"Your physical and emotional feelings are the clues to what needs tending. Allow yourself to feel and express your feelings. Learn to develop a relationship with all parts of yourself so you know what's going on within your being.

"When one part of us isn't working, the whole of us is affected. Welcome back home. You are invited to reconnect with all parts of your precious body, to honor and respond to your feelings, and to listen and respond with the trust of your heart."

The Healing Power of Dis-ease

Sometimes we do not appreciate things until they are broken. The value of something often takes on new meaning when we are without it. I found this to be true with my heart. I had known the delight of love as a human being. The absence of a heart as a Tin Woodman was excessively painful.

I blamed my disheartened life on the Tinsmith and the old woman who had the Witch of the West put a hex on my ax. For a year, I stood empty and powerless. I remained in a state of dis-ease with no attempt to take a deeper look at my role in my experience. I was numb. The only thing I knew was that something was wrong, and I needed it to be fixed.

When Dorothy, Toto, and the Scarecrow found me in the forest, I could hardly respond to myself. I felt almost totally disconnected. Upon learning they were on their way to the Emerald City to see the great Oz, I asked to join them. I wanted to find out if the Wizard could give me a heart.

Through the compassion and love I experienced with these magnificent friends, I regained my senses. I began to take time to reflect on my life. I became conscious that this lack of ease had been a way to bring my attention to repressed pain I had denied for years.

When I finally allowed myself to really feel my emotional pain, the experience caused a deep release. With each new dive into the core of my feelings, I would find another gem of wisdom. These treasures assisted me in getting to the root cause of my disharmony. I began to recognize dysfunctional concepts that had become lodged in my body and inhibited the flow of life's energy. As I let go of these beliefs and attitudes that no longer served me, the flow of life through my body, mind, and emotions stimulated healing.

I developed and nourished new attitudes about what was truly important to me. I learned to listen and respond to the rhythm of life within my very being. I embraced the wonder of life, the miracle of the moment. I found my rhythm and became it.

Having experienced this new level of awareness, I now recognize that when I am feeling out of harmony, it is truly an opportunity to heal another aspect of myself. The next time I experience the lack of ease in my body, I intend to listen more deeply so I can receive the message it is sending.

Emotion, Energy in Motion

Like most boys I heard phrases like:
Don't cry;
Get tough;
You can take it;
Figure it out yourself.

I learned that to *make it* in the world, I needed to control my feelings. I learned to value my mental logic over the wisdom of my heart. *Survival of the fittest* was the name of the game. I had to learn to play by the rules if I wanted to win.

Fortunately, aggression was an acceptable way of expressing emotions. Once I had suppressed an appropriate quantity of sorrow, disappointment, anger, and anxiety, I could channel the whole group of them through aggression. Although it would appear to be an efficient way to deal with emotion, I experienced this avenue as very limiting.

Being in integrity with myself is my commitment. When I look at feelings from a logical point of view, I see that denial of emotion is illogical. My life force is energy in motion, or emotion. For me to deny my emotions is to stifle the flow of life through me. Emotions are neutral, neither good nor bad. They are practical tools for experiencing life.

Over the years I have discovered how to integrate my mind and body with my heart. I have learned to experience the power of an emotion. I can unite the emotion with a thought and create amazing feelings that have opened new worlds for me.

Intimacy, The Ultimate Invitation

For years I kept my distance from anything that even hinted of *relationship*. I had enough heartache to last a life time. I built a grand wall of protection that kept others out quite successfully. Unfortunately, my pain and loneliness remained inside with me.

After a time, I experienced a physical stress upon my heart. I believe the stress was a result of denying my heart love. I cried out for help. My heart responded, "Trust enough to look into me, and you will know intimacy."

My heart guided me to listen to my thoughts, trust my feelings, and respond to my intuitive knowing. Intimacy—Into Me I See. I found that I had never really learned how to have a healthy relationship with myself. To my delightful surprise, I replaced *loneliness* with the *joy of being alone*. I traded in the longing for *someone in my life* for the delight of *being someone in my life*.

Once I experienced intimacy with all dimensions of myself, I no longer needed walls. I naturally set healthy boundaries. I have become committed to being loving, honest, and respectful of myself. This way of being in relationship with myself is profound. This way of being in relationship with others is delightful.

Intimacy is the ultimate invitation to the vastness of love within myself. Into me I see. I like what I see.

Experience the heart in all matter.

Trust the Truth of the Heart

When I lost contact with my heart, I began to mistrust everything, everyone, and myself. I spiraled downward toward despair, searching for some heart strings to grab for security. The friendship of my extraordinary friends in the Land of Oz reactivated my faith in the benevolence of others. They touched my heart deeply with their pure love.

Trusting my feelings was the first step on the way to integrity with myself. It took time for me to regain trust in my feelings because I had disregarded their validity. To engage with my humanity again, I had to embrace my feelings. This sensitive awareness, called feelings, is a unique gift of being human.

The life energy of feelings flows through us just as naturally as blood circulates through the body. The heart is the transformer of the current flow for both of these life conductors. The heart supports the rhythm of life.

When I go to my heart with a question or concern, I know the response I receive is the truth. Since the language of the heart is feelings, it is essential that I develop an understanding of my feelings so my heart and I can communicate clearly.

The resonance of truth I experience when I trust my heart is soothing and powerful. When I embrace my feelings with unconditional love, I honor the wholeness of myself. The heart does not judge the feeling. The heart carries the message so I can feel.

The next level of trust comes forward when it is time to express my feelings. I go again to my heart and trust its discernment, through love, to direct me in the most appropriate expression of the feeling. Trusting the truth of my heart empowers me to feel more freely and love more deeply.

84

The Heart of the Matter

Let us get to the heart of the matter. This is certainly one of the things I learned on my journey—the heart matters. I have a commitment to get to the core of an issue. I go straight to the heart, then proceed forward.

The heart is a miraculous gift. Physiologically, the pulsing rhythm of the heart keeps the life force of blood circulating through our bodies. The heart directs the blood flow out to nourish the body. The blood then returns for purification and regeneration. This amazing process happens automatically. I totally trust the system.

My heart works in partnership with my mind, bringing balance to the linear aspects of decision-making. Using the heart as a touchstone for the mind provides clear thinking and stabilized action.

Another important gift of the heart is the flow of love. As I become more familiar with the movement of the love energy within my system, I can expand the love flow to others. It can then multiply and return to me one hundred fold. It is an amazing experience when I trust my heart and honor its wisdom.

The heart is the cornerstone of my harmony with all levels of myself. It is the vehicle for conscious and profound connection with others. Through my heart I know the universal spirit of love.

The opportunity for living life in a new way is ours. It is time to unclog the chambers of resentment. Time for the shackles of denial to fall away so the love in our hearts can flow freely again. We are the ones to perform this open heart surgery, because we are the ones who closed our hearts.

This is the moment for us to make a new choice. Our life depends on it. Together, let us take the risk to open our hearts to ourselves, to one another, and to love. This is the heart of the matter.

COURAGEOUSLY EMBRACE
YOUR ROYALTY

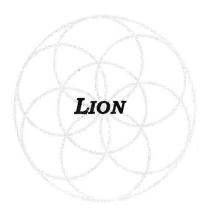

LION

I am the wisdom of royalty that lies within each cell of your body.

Return to Royalty

I am the Lion. I courageously embrace my royalty. I was born into sovereignty. My mother and father were the most regal lions I ever knew. They taught me about my honorable heritage and showed me how to move through the world with grace and strength.

When I was a small cub, tragedy took my beloved parents away from me right before my eyes. For years I wandered the land, frightened and lonely. I lost my courage. The only thing that kept me out of harm's way was my ability to roar.

I was in my deepest despair when Dorothy and her friends crossed my path. I jumped out and roared at them in hope that they would go away and leave me in the safety of my loneliness. Dorothy was not afraid of my size or my roar. She scolded me for frightening her dog.

I told them of the loss of my bravery. I asked to join them on their journey to meet the Wizard and ask him for courage. They accepted me as a fellow seeker and together we overcame many obstacles.

The challenges we faced on the way to the Emerald City called forth my valor and activated memories of my sovereignty. I regained the courage to love and respect myself and reclaim royalty as my birthright. I roar with delight remembering who I really am.

Legacy

My time with my parents was brief, yet powerful. When I was a young cub, I would play and wrestle with my father. He was the honored leader of our pride, our community of lions. Dad would often tell me magnificent stories of great family courage. Mother loved to embellish the tales and remind him of any facts he forgot. They presented me with a rich legacy of love.

My father once said, "You have a great and royal inheritance, my son. The kingdom is within you. You carry the birthright of unlimited potential. Only you can call this power forth."

Being a cub, I did not have enough life experience to understand the expansiveness of what he said, although my core resonated with the truth of his words.

Mother encouraged me to explore the world with strength and grace. "It is your responsibility to find your own roar. As you walk on the earth you will develop your ability to respond to life. With this ability you will know your unique voice of authority."

When I was eight months old, a hunter killed my parents. In terror, I ran away. I attempted to hide from the trauma in the security of separation. The gunshots that took their life blocked my memory of their words of wisdom. I carried tremendous guilt for not saving my parents. This perceived failure damaged my sense of worth and nearly destroyed my belief in my royalty.

For years, I saw myself as a victim of the hunter and lived as if I were the hunted. I used my physical size and my mighty roar to keep others at a distance. *Survival of the biggest*, was my theme. As long as I acted ferocious, I did not have to face my cowardice and feel the deep pain of my loss.

When I met Dorothy and her friends, their determination to find what they were looking for caused me to acknowledge my misery. I realized there was something important I had forgotten; courage was a part of it.

The adventure of traveling with these way-finders ignited a sense of belonging I had not felt for years. The sanctuary of their camaraderie allowed me to develop the courage to experience my pain, honor it, and let it go. I knew that as long as I carried the guilt of "If only I had. . . ," I would destroy myself.

The dangers encountered on the Yellow Brick Road gave me the opportunity to defend the safety of my friends and experience a sense of worth again. As I felt the strength of passion and the power of love, the veil of pain lifted to reveal my legacy. The kingdom lies within, and I found the royal key that unlocks the door.

I embrace my royal heritage.

Courage

For years I abandoned myself and embraced the role of victim. I experienced the world as cruel and terrifying. It seemed that all creation was unsafe, and no matter how small I tried to make myself, the frightening things would always find me.

Some mornings it took tremendous fortitude to get up and begin the day. Survival was my major tool for facing life as I had created it. It was a tormenting experience to lose myself in fear. It seemed my only salvation was to attack the day and all that was in it.

The day I roared at Dorothy's little dog, I met with true heroism. She slapped me on the nose and cried, "Don't you dare bite Toto!" Her daring bravery amazed me.

For the love of her dog, Dorothy dauntlessly stepped into the face of danger. Her valor reminded me that courage is the willingness to live from your core. Being reconnected to this truth returned me to my royal inheritance of love.

In time I was able to perform the most courageous act of my life, forgiving myself for my self-judgments and then forgiving others. My father had told me years earlier, "The courage to be your *royal self* calls forth your unlimited potential."

Fear, True or False

"There's nothing to be afraid of. Don't be scared. You won't be hurt." I had heard these statements from the older lions when I was young. I did not believe them then, and I do not believe them now. There *was* something to be afraid of, and some of it *had* hurt me.

I knew well the survival reactions to fear—fight or flight. The fear I experienced lived within me, and I could neither flee its hold nor battle its power. I knew the face of fear, it visited me in the dark, came alive in my dreams, and embraced me in the light of day. In place of denying the fear, I needed help in knowing how to move through it or let it move through me.

Throughout my life's journey, I have learned fear's rightful place. My instinctual response has saved me in times of physical danger. My intuitive response has taken me beyond the fear to a deeper place within myself. My father once told me that fear always brings a message. "Get out of the way." "Get the threat out of the way," or "Get it, so you can find the way."

My physical instincts take care of the safety of my body. It is the fear that I carry in my mind and emotion that can create even worse destruction. When I remember that fear is the messenger, I do not need to run away. I can face the fear and ask for the message. Once I embrace the true message, I can release the fear and make a choice to move forward with a renewed perception of what is real.

There is a phrase that says fear is "**F**alse **E**vidence **A**ppearing **R**eal." I know that I am the only one who can determine what is false and what is true for me. Once I am clear that through fear I have been seeing false evidence as real, I can replace the fear with love and know the truth. Also, I believe that another purpose of fear is to give us the opportunity as **F**riends to **E**mbrace one **A**nother with the **R**eality of love.

The State of "If Only . . ."

There was a time when I lived my life in the state of, *If only. . .*

If only I had seen the hunter.

If only I had courage.

If only people would respect me.

If only my mane was bigger and my roar was louder.

If only. . .

This state of mind is where I have gone from time to time. It is a place of lack, of not recognizing and appreciating who I am or what I have. I notice that when I focus on what I do not have, I seem to acquire more of it, more of the *lack* that is.

My perception of what is missing in my life is of value. The awareness of what I want to change can move me to determine my new choice. It is wise to make the most of hindsight by using it as a stepping stone to foresight. To notice where I have been and where I am going, without judgment, is profound.

When I weave gratitude between each choice, my kingdom expands. The more I reign over myself with love, respect, and honor, the more I experience life's abundance flowing back to me. I have chosen to release my attachment to the state of *if only* . . . . I joyfully choose living life in the state of grace. Life is much more fun this way.

Find Your Roar

Like most lion cubs, I imitated the sounds I heard from my mother and father. I enjoyed the way each of their voices touched a different place in me. I found tones very fascinating. Every day I would spend hours listening to the various sounds created by life around me.

My playmates would laugh as I attempted to impersonate some of the familiar roars in the neighborhood. It felt magnificent to realize there was a sound that was my roar. I listened intently in each moment, awaiting recognition of a roar I could call mine.

Although Mother appreciated my talent for impersonation, she cautioned me. "It is important that you find your own roar. There is a sound that is your unique voice. It belongs to you and only you. Find your roar, for the world is waiting."

Mother's words became real the day I felt my true roar rise from my core. The tone vibrated with every cell of my being. I knew I had claimed my unique voice. The more awareness I brought to my sound, the more I communicated the spirit of what is important to me. Each roar is a declaration of who I am. The world need wait no longer. I have found my roar.

I Recognize My Pride

It is the nature of lions to associate with others for family living or hunting. My parents and I lived in a pride, a lion community, with two other families. After my parents' death, I left the pride in sorrow and shame because I had not saved them from the hunter.

There was a tearing apart that occurred within me when I left the other lions. My pride in myself was diminished. Being with others only magnified the anguish of losing my mother and father. My solution was to separate myself from anyone or anything that reminded me of my family. I wandered the territory alone, doing what I needed to do to stay alive.

I was in a very vulnerable place when I met Dorothy and her friends. They welcomed me in my defenseless state and accepted where I was in the moment. With them, I felt free to allow my feelings their expression. This willingness to feel my pain and grief gave me strength to move forward and experience life again.

My fellow travelers and I knew our desires. Dorothy wanted to return home, the Scarecrow wanted a brain, the Tin Woodman wanted a heart, and I wanted courage. In this place of naked truth there was a sense of pure power as we joined to accomplish our goals. Our individual ambitions became the common unity for the whole.

Together, we developed courage to face the obstacles along the path to the Emerald City. Collectively, we had the brains to figure things out, the heart to know what was true, and the wisdom to discover a new way of being at home with ourselves. Hand in hand we experienced unconditional love. Our journey together brought us each back to knowing our unique wholeness.

My profound bond with these magnificent companions lives and grows within me today. Their respect and affection guided me to recognizing and returning to my true pride.

Sovereignty of My Kingdom

Being born a lion means being born royal. It is our heritage. There is an innate knowing that we are leaders. Some lions brashly claim their territory and insist that others follow them. My parent's leadership was more by example. They understood that each of us has the potential to be a leader and treated others in that manner. Because of this view of life, there was a great deal of trust in our pride.

My father told me, "You do not have to conquer a territory to have a kingdom. When you are true to yourself and others, your kingdom will come to you."

As I matured, I came to understand this broader concept of dominion. My true kingdom does not lie outside of me. It is the personal realm of my body, mind, and spirit. There is royalty in the thoughts, words and actions I proclaim. To be an authentic ruler of my kingdom, I choose to be consciously responsible. That means using my *ability* to *respond* to any situation while considering the common good of the whole.

Sovereignty is an essential element of a healthy kingdom. To be sovereign means to use my power to govern from within, to be my own authority. In accepting the authority for myself, I agree to take on the authorship of my life, to consciously influence my thoughts and behavior.

Some basic guidelines that I have found beneficial to living the sovereignty of my kingdom are: Clarify my intent or purpose; define my boundaries; love and respect others and myself; balance strength with grace; actively use my ability to respond; and be grateful for the honor of being alive.

CELEBRATE LIFE

WITCH
OF
CELEBRATION

I am the magic of joy
woven within each breath you take.

Magic in Action

I am the Witch of the North. I embody the celebration of life.

When we see life as something to celebrate, MAGIC happens.

When we are in the moment, living happily ever now, a DREAM has come true.

When we allow ourselves to see the weaving of our life experiences, GRACE is recognized.

When we awaken to the awareness that we are the link between Heaven and Earth, a MIRACLE has changed the world.

Come, let us begin, for there is so very much to celebrate.

My First Wand

I inhaled the smell of the rainbow flowers, and wrapped myself in the refreshing moisture of the air. I was about six years old and had gone to the country to visit my grandmother. In the morning I took a walk to sit beside the melodious waterfall. The path along the way was filled with colors and sights that caressed my eyes with radiance.

I saw the devas dancing and heard nature singing in harmony. I embraced the magic of life. I had always felt a oneness with nature. In this place it seemed the spirits were more plentiful and active than anywhere else I'd ever been. I believe that part of it had to do with how much Grandmother loved this sanctuary. Here, she walked, talked, and played with Nature. She had a deep respect for Nature's wisdom. She worked co-creatively with Nature and knew the importance of balance for all.

On this particular day, I was sitting on my favorite rock near the falls. I felt a presence behind me and when I turned around, there stood Grandmother in all her splendor. She would often appear and disappear in the blink of an eye.

"Today is an important day," she began. "You are to open to the magic of love and co-creation in their fullness. As you go through the day, allow your heart, body, mind, and spirit to awaken another level of vibration. In connecting to a deeper level of yourself, you activate your gifts."

She continued, "Nature will see your readiness and move you through the next stages of your process. After you experience the true wonder of the day and receive its bounty, the night shall fall and the sky will present its gift to you. I will then return to give your blessing."

Shivers ran through me knowing that, indeed, this day was magical. I took a deep breath and recalled some of the basics of magic. True magic is co-creative. Divine manifestation happens through conscious partnership with form.

I called upon Nature to join me in co-creating the messenger of my magic, my wand. I asked for guidance on how to begin. I opened my eyes and a butterfly beckoned me to a beautiful Grandmother Sequoia tree. I climbed into the arms of her giant branches, a glorious place of tender strength.

"I am glad you have come," she said. "It is time to awaken the magic within you. Climb among my branches and find the one that is to be your wand."

At first, my heart was so full of amazement that I could not speak. Then I said, "Grandmother Sequoia, your branches are so bountiful, how will I know to choose the right one?"

"That is part of the magic, Dear One. That is the knowing that is awakening in you. Do you have a clear intention of awakening this sacred magic?"

"Yes," leaped from my lips.

"Is your heart pure?"

"Yes."

"Are you willing to take action?"

Taking a deep breath, I responded with "Yes," on the exhale.

"Proceed, you will know what you need to know, when you need to know it."

I closed my eyes and asked the questions of myself so I could feel the certainty of the answer within my whole being.

I asked myself aloud, "Do I have clear intention of awakening the sacred magic within me?"

As I heard the question, chills ran through me. The energy seemed to touch every cell of my being. This was a "Yes," from the physical.

Within my mind, I asked the question a second time. There was a peace of mind that confirmed agreement from my mental body.

I took a deep breath and called upon the core of my spirit. I asked again. The response created a tremendous joy within, matched by a joyful warmth all around. I had confirmed my intention to awaken the sacred magic in me. All dimensions were in alignment.

"Do I have a pure heart?"

The moment I spoke the question, there was a resonance within my body, mind, and spirit that equaled the vibration of a harmonic symphony.

The final question, "Do I have a willingness to take action?"

As soon as the words arose from me, I felt a little tingle of anxiety, along with great excitement. My mind cried, "Awaken the magic." My Spirit resounded, "The magic is awakened."

In that moment, I jumped up and climbed to a branch that seemed to be calling to me. As I got closer to the glistening branch, joy rippled through my body.

"Are you the branch that is to co-create magic with me?"

"I am. I knew you were coming. I've been preparing myself for this day."

"I have been preparing as well," I said. "Do you know our next step?"

"Yes, I have watched this process with brothers and sisters before me. Once there is an agreement between the branch and the witch to be in partnership, the release takes place."

"Little branch, are you willing to work in partnership with me to create magic?"

"I am!"

The moment the branch said, "I am," it released from the Grandmother Sequoia.

I embraced the branch lovingly and cried, "This is marvelous!"

"Just like magic," the little branch responded with a giggle. "I feel different."

"You are different. You've become a wand. It is magic! We agreed to create magic together, and we have!"

Next we went to the place where the golden moss lay. I rolled the wand in the moss to smooth out any rough spots. My toes delighted in the coolness of the moist carpet.

I heard a small voice from a nearby cave, "Hey, over here. Come get me over here."

"What's that, little Witch?" said my new friend, the wand.

"It's coming from the cave. Let's go see," I responded.

As we walked to the cave, I noticed the voice coming from a sparkling deep purple amethyst.

"Hey, I'm to be part of your wand," the purple beauty announced. "I began wondering if you would ever get here. I'm ready for action."

"How will I put you on the wand?" I asked.

"There are three grooves in the branch. I will fit exquisitely in the top one."

Sure enough, I looked at the branch that had magically become my wand. There was an indentation that was a perfect fit for the amethyst.

"Now, touch the wand to that red rose."

As I touched the rose, it opened gently and a beautiful ruby glistened in the light.

"I'm Ruby, at your service," proclaimed the jewel. I picked her up and placed her in the second groove of the wand.

"Where will we find the final jewel?" I asked.

"It will come when it is time," Ruby said.

"What a magical day this has been. I thank each of you for your part in the splendor. It is now time to experience the sacred moment when day turns to night. Let's go to the edge of the world to watch. There is a vast expanse at the top of Sequoia Hill where you can look out to the ocean. It's so magnificent. It is where I love to watch the day gently fade and the night arrive."

As the sun set, I felt the day more fully than I had ever experienced it before. I felt the life of the flowers, trees, birds, ocean, and air in a new way. Brother Sun was on his way to illuminate other worlds. As we watched, we not only saw the magical green flash on the water, there was also a golden afterglow that shot straight to my heart and caused me to exhale.

The sky expressed itself with a celebration of color ending the day and flowing into the night. The transition held serenity and power. I felt I was transforming, too!

In what seemed to be the next moment, there was a silent explosion of light in every part of the sky. The stars took charge of the heavens and announced the night with their twinkles. It was as if I had observed the birth of the night in the same moment I saw the completion of the day. A blanket of quiet peacefulness wrapped around me.

Sister Moon, moving gently from the horizon, joined this celebration of light. As I watched her gracefully rise, I heard her say, "Are you ready for the next step in opening to your magic?"

"This is amazing. The moon is talking to me!"

Sister Moon continued, "You are ready to experience another level of reality. This is your time to awaken to the truth that there is consciousness in energy. That's how magic happens. There is a cooperation or co-creation between energies."

I felt the life of magic within me. There was a place inside that opened up like the unfolding of a lotus. The midnight blue of the sky surrounded me. The light of the stars signaled the reality of magic.

> *Star light, star bright,*
> *I ask to join with you tonight.*
> *My heart is pure, my intention sure.*
> *Awaken the magic,*
> *And with love, it will endure.*

In that moment a shower of light swept across the sky. I felt I was flying with it. I had become as vast as the heavens.

"Hey, down here!" I heard a clear voice.

I looked in my lap, and the brightest star I had ever seen was shining in all its glory. "What are you doing here?" I asked.

"You made a wish didn't you?"

"Yes," I acknowledged.

"Well, I'm Star Bright, and I'm here to be a part of your magic. Place me at the end of the wand. With this action we unite day and night, Heaven and Earth, light and dark. We become wholeness in action. Some call this magic, we know it simply as *truth*."

My whole being vibrated as if I were a tuning fork. I closed my eyes and entered into the realm of sleep. There was so much to integrate. In my dream state I saw Grandmother. She touched me gently and said, "Awaken, my child a new life is yours."

I opened my eyes to see her standing before me. The love she radiated caused a surge of energy to move through my heart, shooting vertically through my body. I felt stretched from my heart to the core of the Earth and the heights of Heaven simultaneously.

Grandmother laid a cloth spun of gold at my feet. "Place your wand on the sacred cloth," she directed.

I did so with great reverence.

"This emerald is the third and final jewel in your wand. It comes from the Emerald City as a reminder that true magic comes from the heart. In this moment I acknowledge the co-creation that has taken place between Nature, the Universe, and you. This is a partnership as powerful as the love that created the world. As a representative of this truth, I bless you and your sacred wand. Through the power of your love, the wand is activated."

I then picked up my wand and proclaimed, "I promise to work in harmony with the source of life to support those who are ready to receive their heart's desire."

Expectations Get in the Way

One of the challenges of being a witch is dealing with the expectations people have of you. No, I choose to reframe that statement. One of the challenges of being a witch is being at peace with yourself, so that the expectations of others does not affect you.

No doubt about it, others' expectations used to influence me. I once thought that one aspect of being a witch was doing things to please people so they would like me. It was important to be sought after. Therefore, I would go to extremes to assist people in getting their wishes granted. I would often work 18-hour days and take requests in the middle of the night. Unfortunately, I reached the point of exhaustion before I finally realized I was letting expectations get in the way of being my true magical self.

My expectations of myself were the first limits of judgment that I released. Facing these presumptions allowed me to readily see assumptions others had of me.

People have a common misconception that they simply make a wish and I come forward to grant it. This expectation of being an *instant wish granter* has been a challenging one for me. Not because I do not love granting wishes, but because wish granting is a partnership. It is the co-creative effort between us that manifests the desired outcome.

The urge to wish is magical and comes from a deep place within our soul. There are four things that must be in place for the granting of a wish: Clear intention; pure heart; openness to receive; and willingness to take action. When we see life as something to celebrate, rather than something to manipulate, magic happens.

115

Granting Wishes

For years I granted wishes to anyone who would ask. Believe me, there were plenty who asked! It was as if I were some kind of instant wish-vending dispenser. That is certainly how it began to feel.

Now, it was not always like that. I remember when I received my first wand. Things seemed more magical then. People believed in their goodness and treated life with more respect and wonder. The call for magic came from people with a pure heart and a wise soul. The granting of a wish was a sacred expression of Divine Love. I treated it as such.

Everyone was aware that calling upon the skills of the Wise Woman was an act of surrender. When joining with clear intention, the manifestation was instantaneous.

As a young witch, I was schooled well in the gracious service of others. It was my purpose to be present to others and grant them their heart's desire. It was glorious work, but I had forgotten one of the major lessons: "Granting wishes to others comes from the overflow of granting wishes to yourself."

I had not been honoring myself, so I began to feel resentment toward others. I had allowed my service to become sacrifice. As my resentment grew, so did the apparent disregard of my service by those who wanted wishes granted.

There was no partnership in creating the magic anymore. There was a desire for instant gratification without participation. It was ugly.

One day, I realized that my wand did not have the spark that it used to. The granting of wishes was becoming difficult. At that point I placed my wand into the crystal chamber for cleansing and I went to the purification pools. As I looked into the waters, I saw what I had become—a witch out of touch with her own goodness. It was as if I were an empty shell.

I spent three days at the sacred pools and reconnected with the truth of magic—it flows because I use it first for myself. The more I access the magic, the more I have to share with others.

Because I was in such a depleted state, I had called others to me who had faded resources. They wanted me to do all the work. I had fallen out of partnership with myself, therefore, I could not work in partnership with others.

Thank goodness for the purification pools! That experience of renewal was one of the best wishes I was ever granted. It is great to feel my vibrant self again.

Star Power

It is very significant that a star crowns my magic wand. A simple wand is for Earth magic. A star-tipped wand is for activating celestial power upon the Earth.

There is an aspect of us that looks to the stars and makes a wish, that strives for visions beyond our reach and knows the truth of hope realized. The star on my wand represents the proclamation that we have the opportunity to make a higher potential active within us.

We remember our divine creation through this light of the heavens. The star invites us to stand with our head erect, our arms and legs outstretched, and become a living star on Earth. In this powerful and open stance, we can recognize the sacredness of ourselves. We can receive the gifts of light from the Earth and the heavens.

There are some days when I feel the power of this celestial connection and others when I am alone in a void. In these void moments, I feel separated from the promise of the stars and disengaged from the core of myself.

It is my innate desire to connect. Therefore, when I sense disunity, I take action. I reengage with myself by taking a deep breath. I place my hands palm up at my side, and state my intention to reconnect with star power. As I raise my hands slowly up to the sky, I become aware of my connection with all living things.

Once my hands reach the sky, I place fingertip to fingertip, blending the energy of the sky to that of the Earth. I feel the heartbeat of the Earth and the pulsing of the stars in my fingertips. As I bring my star-tipped hands to my solar plexus, I breathe in the Oneness of all creation. This renewed awareness of the light shines brightly within me, and I embrace the gift of star power.

I celebrate the magic that is me.

Celebrate Life with Gratitude

"Gratitude is the true magic of life. When the awareness of life's profoundness awakens in your soul, celebration becomes your essence." These words of my grandmother still echo in my mind and reverberate in my heart.

Grandmother was a master teacher of sacred magic, and she lived to honor and celebrate life. As we walked together, she would often sing the song called *Feel the Magic.*

> *Feel the magic of life within you.*
> *See the magic of life around you.*
> *Hear the magic of life flow through you.*
> *Touch the magic of life that renews you.*
> *Be the magic of life, and choose to*
> *Celebrate the magic that is you.*

All of life celebrates its existence in one form or another. We can learn from the birds who sing in a new day, and the flowers that express their joy in many different colors and forms. Each day, the sun announces a new beginning and the moon offers the calm of the night. Trees gift us with oxygen to breathe. The ocean reminds us to play as it dances to and from the shore. The mountains reflect our majesty.

It is a natural phenomenon to celebrate who we are, to show our colors, to shine our light, to sing our song. It may be that your innate desire to celebrate life has not experienced nurturing or recognition. It is possible that circumstances have been such that resentment is more familiar to you than gratitude. If this experience of life has been your reality, I am here to let you know that, in this moment, you can make a new choice. This instant can be the one in which you make the decision to recreate life as something to celebrate.

When I forget the beauty of life within me and spiral down to a suffocating place of judgment, I take a breath. The first step back to honoring life is to take a conscious breath. As I inhale, I infuse my body with the new life I am choosing and release that which no longer serves me. With the second breath, I express gratitude for being able to receive and release with the breath.

I love the delight of feeling the pulse of life in every part of my body. I am grateful for my ability to see, hear, touch, and know. I drink in these precious presents of life. It is a miracle to *be*, and an honor to *love*. I rejoice in the life that flows through me and appreciate the essence of all existence. I consciously choose to celebrate my life each day, for if I do not, who will?

Sacred Focus, Not Hocus-Pocus

Magic was a way of life in our home. We honored the sacred power of focused energy. We understood that we are more than physical beings. Even as children, we knew we only used our gifts in cooperation with Nature and the heavens.

Friends, not of our cultural heritage, sometimes interpreted our ways as hocus-pocus. The magic they were familiar with was sleight of hand enchantment. That type magic embraces the art of illusion. It can provide trickery in a form that creates much enjoyment for the observer.

There is a tendency to disbelieve that which we do not comprehend. Sacred Magic is beyond intellectual understanding. Our magic does not deal with false impressions. This sacred wisdom interacts with a broader knowledge of reality. Sacred Magic is the act of consciously becoming One with the pure essence of something in order to work harmoniously in manifesting a change. Arrogance has no place in Sacred Magic. We always work in relationship and ask permission from the person or thing with which we are interrelating. This is an honoring of the consciousness that lives in all forms.

Elders pass on this sacred wisdom through demonstration of their true enlightenment. Although there are ancient guidelines, this level of magic vibrates beyond a static formula. It is never written down. It is lived. I learned by observing, listening, and intuiting from my place of knowing.

This wisdom of ages moves through me in a manner uniquely different from my mother and grandmother. For me to truly be a Witch of Celebration, it is imperative that

I honor the charm of life that flows through me. The mastery of my individual expression expands the integrity of the whole. Our sacred focus has been, and always will be, to have reverence for all life and to choose to co-create through love. Indeed, Sacred Magic is focus, not hocus-pocus.

Where Heaven and Earth Meet

There is a sacred place where Heaven and Earth meet. In this space of holiness, the power of co-creation between these two is manifest. The location of this divine meeting is in the heart of humanity. Yes, Heaven and Earth lie within the heart of you.

As a being who interacts with the sacred energy of creation and sees relationships from a universal perspective, I acknowledge your precious gift of being Spirit in human form. I have observed that sometimes you get so caught up in your perception of what is important that you are blind to the true wonder of your being. You are often deaf to the nurturing heartbeat of the Earth and the music of the heavens that vibrates in your every breath.

I invite you to awaken to the sacred union of Heaven and Earth within you. It is time to recognize your intimate relationship with Nature and remember the wisdom of Heaven that lies within your soul. This celebration of love is ready to radiate from your core the moment you consciously honor the gift.

Being a child of the Universe is a sacred heritage. Approach this legacy with humility. Step forward into your heart with grace and claim this miraculous inheritance of love. The magic of life lies in the wisdom and understanding of embracing one's role in this great miracle.

Honor your inheritance from Mother Earth and Father Sky by renewing your relationship with their wisdom. I invite you to step forward to be Love on the Earth. There are many who join you on this journey to remembering your heritage. I am here as the Witch of

Celebration to participate in this grand, gala event of your awakening to the miracle that you are. Let the celebration begin!

ACCEPT RESPONSIBILITY
FOR
SELF-TRANSFORMATION

WITCH
OF
TRANSFORMATION

*I am the magic of transformation
dancing through your being.*

Sweeping Discoveries

I am the Witch of Transformation. You may remember me as the Wicked Witch of the West from the Land of Oz. When I met Dorothy, I was at the height of my evil period, and the entire land loathed me. The loving resolve of this little girl to find her way home was the ultimate power that dissolved my wickedness.

I am a renewed witch now. I have lots to share about my journey of transformation. I understand some of you may choose not to engage with me for fear of contamination. I honor your choice. Another perspective I will offer is that, as you stand in judgment of the way I was, you may be sitting in judgment of some aspect of yourself.

This invitation to interact with me is an opportunity to walk safely through doors you may have closed long ago, to recover a transcendent part of yourself. I know a great deal about judging others and myself. Over the years I became all that I had judged. It was an ugly and unhappy existence.

Once my wicked self dissolved, I began experiencing my true form. I now accept responsibility for my self transformation and have replaced my judgmental nature with discernment through love. This discovery of self-transformation, is clearly the point of my journey. I bid you to take a loving risk for yourself and join me in my tales of transformation. You may discover something you are ready to sweep out of your life in order to embrace a fuller aspect of your magnificence.

Living on the Offense

Abandoned as the infant of a witch, I learned early to fend for myself. In our tract, they called me a stray. Other young witches would taunt me and attempt to place offensive spells on me. Revenge arose from my pain, and I chose to come out fighting at every turn.

To be the most feared, wickedest witch around became my sole purpose. I chose to accept that I might be worthless, and I took it to the extreme. I would turn people against me or push them away before they could reject me. Although the result of *exclusion* was the same, I had the twisted satisfaction of feeling in control.

For a great deal of my life, this illusion of power over others satisfied my desire to feel important. Of course, the truth was that people did what I demanded because they were afraid of me. They held me in no more esteem than I did myself.

Irreverence for others, irreverence for life, and irreverence for myself was a painful existence. It was like being in a revolving door that consistently takes you back to the isolation you are attempting to escape.

Living on the offense is debilitating. I do not recommend it.

Shadow Self

I spent most of my life feeling sad, disconnected, angry, and lost. Somehow, the familiarity of that which ached was comforting. My life experience had trained me to believe my shadow-self was the real me. The more people treated me as a cast-off, the more incorrigible I became. I believed this ghost of darkness and I were one.

The day that Dorothy from Kansas tossed water on me, a death occurred. She intended to save her friend, the Scarecrow, and her act of love dissolved the wicked, contemptible part of myself.

In my liquefied state, I realized there was a piece of me that did not shrink away. Although everyone had deserted me, I heard a voice echo in the castle, "Your true self remains. That which you created through self judgment was washed away. You now have a new choice. You can hold onto the illusion that you are worthless, or you can embrace the light that you are and transform life as you have known it. The choice is yours."

Spontaneously I cried out, "I choose transformation!" There was an energy more powerful than a lightning bolt that shot through me. When I opened my eyes, I was lying on the floor in a puddle of water. Upon arising, I slowly walked to the mirror and saw a face more radiant than I had ever before known. I looked deeply and lovingly into the eyes looking back at me and said, "I choose life."

Each day became a new beginning. I let go of judgment and learned to honor the whole of me, the light and the shadow. I discovered how to lovingly embrace my shadow-self and listen to the message it was bringing. I continue to uncover shadow places within me and to illuminate the spaces. When my shadow-self appears, it is often because I have stepped between the light and myself.

How Did You Get to be So Ugly and Wicked?

When I was at the prime of my self-destruction, a curiosity seeker asked, "How did you get to be so ugly and wicked?"

Since it had been my intention for people to know me as heartless and incorrigible, I initially took the inquiry as a compliment. Later, I realized I resented the comment regarding my lack of good looks. Therefore, I put a short term spell on the fellow for referring to me as ugly.

The question he had posed reverberated over and over in my mind. It had pierced my exterior as if a dagger and exposed my hidden spaces to light. Questions I had long ago banished to the silent darkness demanded an answer. "From where did wickedness come? Was ugliness part of my heritage? Was this state of being what I really wanted?"

The reflection of these questions was terribly painful. Their release from their safe imprisonment enraged me. I demanded that this chatter stop and slammed the door on the thoughts, hoping they would never find their way to the surface again.

After the melting away of my wicked self, these questions sat waiting for my attention. I was now ready to respond. As I entered into relationship with each question, I discovered that it had been my choice to bury my anger, judgment, resentment, and jealousy deep inside. Over time these emotions had fermented and filled me with rottenness that infected my whole body. I developed warts, my back became hunched and my hair was a brittle, unruly mess. The spoilage infiltrated my attitude and actions, and triggered the worst in others. It was a circle of viciousness that began with self-judgment.

Now, I have a sense of freedom. I allow myself to ask questions and know the truth of the answers. I shall forever be grateful to that inquiring stranger for the thought he planted years ago. I have learned that the more questions I ask of myself, the more I blossom.

The Flight of Fright

I was horrid in my wickedness. The only thing that mattered was getting my way. I did not care whom I hurt or what I had to do to acquire what I wanted. I used the charm of the Golden Cap to manipulate the Winged Monkeys. I sent them to terrorize Dorothy and her companions and bring me the magic slippers. The Monkeys became fright in flight, and their mischievous behavior evoked grand anxiety.

In those days, creating mayhem was my calling card. I relished the control I felt by causing chaos. When an external event aroused a person's inner doubt or fear, there was a rippling effect that often disabled them. The Winged Monkeys were very good at creating such distress. Their ability to tear apart or capture a victim was frightening.

Although my wicked days are behind me, I continue to realize the power of fear. Fear gives us a vivid reference point, marking where we are in relationship to where we desire to be. Our ability to react defensively or offensively to something that may harm us is a very important skill. On the other hand, dysfunction can occur when we carry so much fear within us that we project our anxiety and see Winged Monkeys everywhere.

We are not separate from fear, anymore than we are separate from love. They both reside within us. It is how we choose to interact with these energies that makes the difference.

Fear can hold us in bondage, or fear can be a guardian that calls forth the power of love to support us. Love can free us from polarity and return us to a balanced integration within ourselves and, in turn, within the whole.

We hold the charm of authority to free our fright. As we more fully embrace the divinity of the whole, our love soars on wings of delight.

Stop the World, I'm Out of Here!

I have had moments when I wanted to run through the world screaming, "Stop, I want to get off!"

The external and internal pressures can become so intense that I feel I am spinning out of control. I want to grab hold of the world and slow it down, or simply jump off into the silent void. In my drama queen era, I attempted both solutions. I am here to testify that neither of them were successful.

I discovered that it serves me better when I slow myself down. Then, I can re-create my world moment by moment and connect with the rhythm of the Earth, rather than the erratic energy of some of her inhabitants.

Chaos is a gift I honor. It moves me to another level of self-understanding. Now, when I become caught up in life's turmoil, instead of running through the streets, I allow myself to run through my mind, crying out, "Stop the world, I'm out of here." This freedom of expression releases the frustration and takes me right to the center of the disorder. In this calm, I can face the true issue within me that has vibrated so loudly to get my attention.

When I lovingly listen to the aspect of myself that feels in trauma, there is a shift in my world. Embracing myself with compassion allows me to see my wholeness in the process of expanding.

Indeed, I am the world and the world is me. As I continue to experience harmony within myself, the balance that exists in the world around me becomes more clear. It is through compassion that I can invite myself to step back into the world and be a conscious part of keeping it tenderly turning.

New Days are Born of Darkness

I have known days of darkness and empty nights. I have known a life of fear and separation. Because I have known these things, I can choose to live beyond these experiences.

New days are born of darkness. It is a passage important in the cycle of life. The trouble comes when I become stuck in the dark and forget the balance. There were times when I had feelings of anger, resentment, and jealousy. I judged my feelings and put them in a dark place within me, hoping they would somehow go away. They did not. They just got denser because I piled other emotions on top of them.

This composting of feelings can be a messy business. Judgment, denial, guilt, and shame are catalysts for further decay of suppressed emotions. The thoughts that hold this compression of feelings are judgment and arrogance. When I let go of self-condemnation, light pierces through the density.

It was these dark days that helped me discover my life was worth fighting for. I learned about my strength and tenacity, about my ability to focus on surviving in that reality. As I grew from surviving into thriving, I began using my magic in a more illuminated manner.

My magic dwells in the west, the place where the sun sets, where the darkness puts the day to rest so a new beginning can take place. The dark of night brings the gift of silence as a place to reflect on the activity of the day. The rhythm of the night offers a slowing down that is important to balance. I can now enter the dark of night and embrace the peace that awaits me. Because I have known the darkness, I can choose the day with new appreciation.

As we more fully embrace the divinity of the whole,
our love soars on wings of delight.

"Surrender, Dorothy"

When I wrote "Surrender, Dorothy" across the sky, I wanted her to give the magic slippers to me. I was living a win / lose life and her surrender would mean, I had won. That polarized thinking came from a limited mind.

I let go of duality at the time of my dissolution and expanded my view of life. From this broader system of thinking, I know that no one can truly win until we work in unity. Initially, giving up the illusion of dualism was frightening. As I learned to embrace both the shadow and the light aspects of myself, I opened up to *all* that I am. Surrendering old habits, beliefs, attitudes, and behaviors that had their foundation in fear was the most powerful and profound experience in my life.

I understand that true surrender means to release that which no longer serves me. It is an experience of freedom to surrender the unfolding of my life to the vast mystery of the sweet whole.

With a new outlook, I write across the sky for all to see, "Surrender!" It is the best advice I will ever give. It is the greatest gift I have ever received.

Transformation, a Personal Responsibility

I was born a witch with free will. I evolved my unethical behavior one thought, one word, one action at a time. From a place of fear, anger, and resentment, I used my magic to harm others. I lived in this state of indignation and self-sabotage for years and experienced the painful consequences of my arrogance. Life was as I had created it.

My experience of dissolving into a pool of water was a rude awakening that provided me an opportunity to make some new choices. In this fresh place of awareness, I wanted to transform the way I had been. Unlike shape-shifting, transformation is more than one-stop shopping for a new look. This change was an inside job that required total commitment.

My first step was to re-engage in a loving relationship with myself. This was most difficult because my life was based on fear. The power that moved me forward was a conscious choice and clear intent to go beyond my present form to a fuller expression of my vastness. Once aligned with love, I released the mutated aspects of myself and was able to step through a new door to continue my journey of transformation.

Metamorphosis requires full integrity with each step. From egg, to larva, to cocoon, each stage must unfold naturally for the birth of the butterfly. Even though there is an organic process in metamorphosis, conscious participation with each stage is essential.

In partnership with the mystery of my wholeness, I created a new blueprint for my thoughts, my words, and my actions. Each day I lovingly respond to life from a place of sacred fidelity. Transformation is an enlightening experience that dances through my being.

The Gift of Vulnerability

There is a place called vulnerability that I avoided most of my life. I focused on exposing others' shortcomings and meddling in their affairs. This preoccupation with creating misery for others helped me elude facing myself.

Dorothy's bucketful of water baptized me into the grace of vulnerability. After my initial disorientation, I found this place of naked truth almost comforting. It was a space of no pretense, no expectations, no fears—simply, pure *being*.

In this experience of open abandonment, I inhaled the unconditional love that had been patiently awaiting my reception. Compassion embraced fragments of myself that self-judgment had separated. I felt clarity, and a renewed sense of life.

Surrendering to my vulnerability proved to be a profound awakening. I experienced a link between my conscious and unconscious awareness that sent a current of light through my entire being. I reclaimed my soul, reactivated my heart, renewed my body and reviewed my mind. With all my systems calibrated and united, the miracle of my life's vitality could come into its true form. A precious gift unfolded from this place of humble wisdom. The treasure presented itself through a powerful voice within me saying,

Go forward from this day and remember:
Intend love, intuit truth, and integrate wisdom.

DEMONSTRATE THE
WISDOM AND POWER OF LOVE

WIZARD

*I am the wisdom of power that
lies at the core of your love.*

Wizdom Remembered

I am the Wizard. I know the wisdom and power of love.

I am a common man who for years pretended to be a great and powerful Wizard. I controlled people through activating their fear and manipulating their imagination.

A little dog named Toto exposed me. I felt the delight of freedom that day because I had been hiding behind illusion for a long time. Even though I had been deceitful, Dorothy and her friends forgave me. That experience of compassionate acceptance awakened my understanding of the power of love and the wisdom of putting love into action.

As I embraced the courage to use my heart in all matters, I unlocked a great memory bank of true wisdom. I now recognize and claim that I am indeed a Wizard of Love in the form of a man.

In Search of the Wizard Within

Mystic wonders, extraordinary adventures, enchanted lands, and the wisdom of ages have been fascinations of mine since I was a boy. On a warm Nebraska summer night, I would lie in the cool grass and study the stars. I would dream about other times and places, wonder about the knowledge in the heavens, and long to travel the Universe.

I became a ventriloquist and later a balloonist. With these skills I could travel most anywhere and be looked upon as a bit of a Wizard. One day while in my balloon, the ropes got tangled, and I was unable to direct the craft. I flew high above the clouds for over a day. The balloon floated on the air currents far beyond familiar territory, lulling me to sleep. Upon awakening, I discovered I was traveling over an unknown and beautiful country. The balloon landed in the midst of a group of astonished people. My arrival from the heavens mystified them, and they assumed I was a Wizard. It was as if I had landed in the middle of my childhood dreams. I was ready to play the part.

Much to my surprise, the people were afraid of me and took action on any request I made. I ordered them to build a city and create a palace for me. My directive was that the city be adorned with the most beautiful of everything. The people were happy and they liked me. I was a good Wizard and directed the people to engage in work that brought them delight.

In the quiet seclusion of the palace, I would often reflect on how I was using illusion as a controlling mechanism. I hungered for the nourishment of true knowledge and power. I spent many hours investigating

148

astrology and reading about the lives of mystics. I desired to study with Masters and be versed in ancient wisdom so I could be an authentic Wizard.

The arrival of Dorothy and her determined friends helped me understand that my quest is the same search many are on. There appears to be a desire in us to find the Wizard, the Teacher, the Guru or the Priest. We want answers to our questions, resolve brought to our problems, and knowledge of hidden wisdom. It is an important journey, because there are clearly questions to be answered, problems to be resolved, and wisdom to be discovered.

Dorothy, Toto, the Scarecrow, Tin Woodman, and the Lion served as my teachers. They awakened my wizardry by challenging me to delve into my own wisdom to assist them. There are many master teachers along the way, if we open our hearts, minds, and souls to experience them. They may not appear in the form we had imagined or give the answers we desired. If they have directed us to search within ourselves for knowledge, they have served the role of wizard.

In this present time, I know myself as student and master. I continue to discover the mystic wonders, extraordinary adventures, enchanted lands, and wisdom of ages within the depths of myself. I honor all that I know and all that is yet to be known. Through the wisdom of love, I have found the Wizard I was looking for, and it is me.

No More Hiding Behind
Curtains, Veils, or Blindfolds

There was a time in my life when I hid from the world and myself. I created an illusion of authority to frighten others while I concealed my true essence. I was a wizard of disguises, and I manipulated people through fear. I purposely kept others at a safe distance. I wanted no one to know that I was merely a man.

When Dorothy and her friends came to see "The Wizard," Toto pulled the curtain back and exposed me. At first, I was angry and embarrassed, then I experienced a big sense of relief. I did not have to continue to pretend to be something I wasn't.

They forgave me my indiscretions, and a veil of deception lifted from my heart. I immediately remembered that the true wizardry of wisdom lies within. With that awareness, I recognized the Knowledge of the Scarecrow, the Pure Heart of the Tin Woodman, and the Royal Courage of the Lion. As I acknowledged and honored each of them for who they are, I experienced more of my grandeur. In letting go of playing a role that had defined me falsely, my eyes were free to see true mastery in myself and in all those around me.

In this time of ultimate exposure:

    All curtains are drawn.

    All veils are lifted.

    All blindfolds are removed and justice is served.

    For that is who we are,

    Just Us,

    The magic of Love in many forms

The time is now to be only love.

Authentic Power is Love

As a Wizard, I have observed a great deal about the dynamics of power within myself and within others. In the Emerald City, I had the opportunity to play with power in my limited understanding of its essence. The potency of experiencing unconditional love as true power cracked me open to the core. This exposure allowed a space for old beliefs to leave and for original truths to evolve.

If I were to announce that you could come to me today and receive power, people would line up, anticipating the reception of different things. A wealthy person might expect to acquire more money, a politician status, an academic knowledge, and an entertainer fame. These forms of energy are not where true power lies, although they are often seen as power tools.

Genuine power is far more vast than many can conceive. Authentic power is the pure essence of love. Its true potential lies beyond the authority of the physical realm. When we weave pure love into money or fame, this interrelationship can have immeasurable positive influence.

I hold myself accountable for being conscious about how I use my wizardry. A key question I always ask myself is, "For what purpose do I intend to use my influence?" If the answer is anything different from "Only love," I do not take action.

With real power as my focus, I move forward from my heart, listen to the wisdom of my soul and experience that:

Authentic Love is Power. - *Authentic Power is Love.*
The Power of Love is Authentic.

152

The Wizard's Grace

I know the techniques of *sleight of hand* trickery and illusionary reality. I have used this art of third dimensional manipulation to both entertain and deceive. Although I enjoyed the novelty of my actions, I desired to experience wizardry as a master, rather than as a manipulator.

In my commitment to become a more accomplished Wizard, I went in search of the soul of magic. The word *magic* has its derivation from the Greek word *magikos* which means *of the Magi*. These *wise men* were extraordinary because they integrated their inner spiritual guidance with the knowledge they gained from observing nature and the heavens. So too, the mastery of Merlin originated from a spiritual place of wisdom. These expanded beings helped me see that real magic has its source in the grace of love.

I have chosen to fully embrace my gift of wizardry. In love, I invited grace to carry me to the divine wisdom of my soul, to unite me with the divine wisdom of nature, and to open me to the divine wisdom of the heavens. Weaving grace throughout my every thought, word, and action has created a spirit of enchantment in my life. I continue to unfold my power and wisdom of love and experience delight in the magic of each moment.

Like the air we breathe, grace surrounds us and flows through us. Our part is to acknowledge it, to take it in, and allow it to weave in and out of every aspect of who we are. There is grace in magic. There is magic in grace. Let us live our lives from this magical place of grace.

The Magic of Oz

The land of Oz is a place of enchantment. The Emerald City lies at the creative center of this charmed country, as the heart lies at my center. My life here has been *oz*-inspiring. It has taken years for me to comprehend that the Magic of Oz is the *wisdom of wholeness*.

I know that wholeness, along with the journey back to remembering it, is all there is. My sojourn has taken me deep into the mystery of myself. In this holy space, I experienced *love* as the life blood of wholeness. With each forward step I take, I carry the magic of Oz within the essence of who I am. I see with *emerald eyes*, the eyes of love. I view the world and my experiences in it through this powerful wisdom. It is with this vision that I truly embrace my holiness and experience the whole of which I am a part.

There is a phrase on American currency, *E Pluribus Unum*. It means "many make the one" or "one out of many." This statement reflects the conscious intent to be a country based on the *wisdom of wholeness*. This request to the *many* to become the *One,* is the current higher calling of this time.

I realize that this call to wholeness has been an urging within me for most of my life. I had been living in a disconnected relationship with many aspects of myself. I now acknowledge the power of each dimension: Body, mind, heart, and spirit. The whole is stronger than the sum of the parts. In this broader place of self awareness, that which has separated me from others ceases to exist. The truth of Oneness is becoming more familiar.

I have chosen to live my life from a deeper place within myself. Love empowers my decision-making. I base my life on the knowledge that what I choose affects every living thing. As I continue on my journey of this Golden Wizdom, many others join me who remember the Magic of Oz, the *wisdom of wholeness*.

Invitation to Mastery

As the Wizard of Oz, I invite you to step into the Mastery of You. Be your own alchemist by taking that which may appear to be the basic elements of life and turning them into your wizdom of gold.

Each of us brings a unique piece of wholeness to the life of the planet. Our conception was our invitation to be in mastery of our piece of the wholeness. There is no one else that brings life to form as you do. You are the one and only expert of your body, mind, heart, and soul.

The time is *now* to activate the original intent. The time is *now* to be only love, for that is who we are. The unification of ancient wisdom with the new co-creative technology of wholeness is upon us. It is within us. Let us embrace this technology of wholeness within ourselves. We can research the quantum physics of love, consciously co-create with Nature, and resonate with the music of the spheres. Let us time travel by being in the moment, shape shift by reconnecting with the purpose of our soul, and interact with the wisdom of the stars.

Our invitation to celebrate this divine mastery is here. Activating the mastery in each of us is essential for the expansion of the whole. Our choice to live in the genius of our mastery makes a profound difference to all that is, from the smallest quarks to the largest universe in the cosmos. It is our time to show up in our fullness, to live in our wholeness.

Activate Love

There is a power within you beyond measure.

There is a power within you awaiting your recognition for full activation.

There is a power within you awaiting your remembering for full celebration.

Reconnect

Remember

Receive

Respond to the power within.

Know this power of

LOVE.

Know that You are

THE POWER OF LOVE IN ACTION.

GOLDEN TOUCHSTONES

MASTERS OF OZ

We are the Oneness that lies within the many aspects of you.

One Out of Many

At first glance, our wayfaring group appears to be as diverse as any gathered. Just picture it—a little girl, her dog, a scarecrow, a tin man, and a lion interacting with little people, witches, and a wizard. How could such a conglomeration accomplish anything?

The answer is, through unconditional love. We each had a personal commitment to our heart's desire and a willingness to compassionately support one another in achieving our intent. There was a common union that took place and strengthened our mutual vision. Through our interactions and adventures we awakened aspects in one another that had been latent. We stepped into the wholeness of our unique selves. We expanded to becoming *one whole body* of unique beings joined for a common purpose. We became a Council of One Out of Many.

The journey to the Emerald City is about awakening to the magnificence of who we truly are. It is an opportunity to gather those aspects of ourselves that we believe are separate from us. The Emerald City is where we realize the heart of *all matter*. It is the place where the integration of all aspects of ourselves unite.

In coming to closure with this part of our journey, we realize another spiraling adventure has already begun. As we consciously choose to live our wholeness solely through love, a door opens that leads us to a golden path *beyond* the Emerald City. We step forward with integrity and live the Golden Wizdom we discovered individually and collectively.

As individuals and as a Council, we are grateful to have had this opportunity to share our fascination with life from our personal points of view. We acknowledge your journey and the choices you have made along the way. We invite you to continue to live in the knowing that home lies within; unconditional love is in the moment; thoughts create; truth lies in your heart; you are royal; life is to celebrate; self-transformation is a personal responsibility; and, there is wisdom and power in love.

When people return home from a journey, they often bring gifts for those they love. Our gifts to you are fifty *Golden Touchstones*. A touchstone was formerly used to determine the purity of gold. The gold would be rubbed across the surface of the black stone and the color of the resulting streak would determine the gold's value. These *Golden Touchstones.* are words to serve as a reminder of the purity of your essence, and your immeasurable value. The treasure of these gifts unfolds the moment you accept the present.

*The Oz experience
is a journey
to wholeness.*

*Everyone
is on their way
somewhere.*

*Each life experience
is unique, yet there is a
resonance of similarity.*

The call to awaken

comes

in many forms.

*Find the heart
of the matter
and proceed forward.*

Allow time and space
for golden wizdom
to become you.

The most profound
relationship
is the one
you have
with yourself.

Compassion
unites the many
to One.

The magic of life

lies

in divine simplicity.

Ozmosis

is the loving art

of becoming my Being

in the flowing presence

of that which is your

Being.

*Once you embrace
your heart's desire,
you see life through
Emerald Eyes,
the eyes of love.*

Honest inner action
nurtures
powerful interaction.

The journey through life

is

holy / whole-ly work.

It's your story,

live it

with authenticity.

It is no longer

appropriate

to pretend

you do not know

who you are.

The Yellow Brick Road
is an opportunity
to remember your Self.

Integrity arises through the integration of body, mind, heart and spirit.

Clear intention creates

a space for

clear manifestation.

**Be mindless
at least
once a day.**

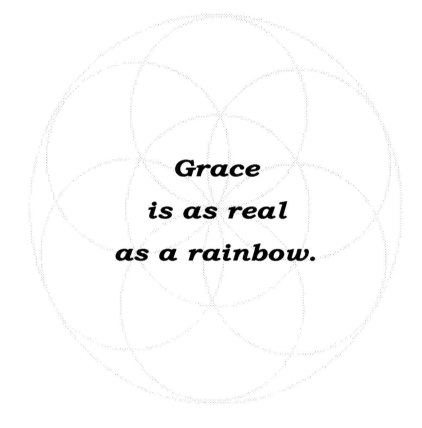

*Grace
is as real
as a rainbow.*

Golden Wizdom

is accessed

through the heart.

The path ahead
is one we will take
together.
It is a path of
conscious participation.

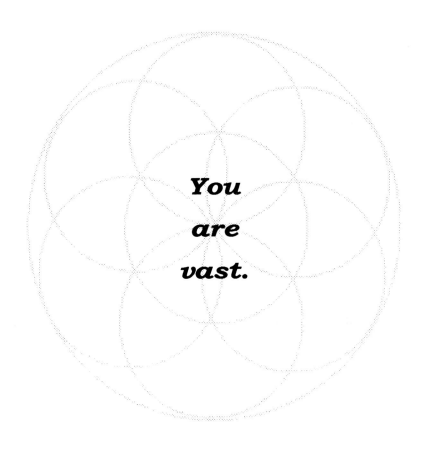

You
are
vast.

*You are invited
to live beyond
that which you thought
was the goal.*

*When you see life
as something to celebrate,
MAGIC happens.*

Conscious choice is active.
You choose,
fine tune,
and choose again.

Co-creation multiplies options.

Touch your life,
and you touch
the life of another.

Intend love,
intuit truth,
and integrate wisdom.

Partner with your spirit

in the

spiraling dance of life.

*The vastness
of who you are
can embrace
joy and sorrow
in the same moment.*

*Honor
the diversity of others,
it will enhance your life.*

Make choices

in the

conscious state of Oz.

*When you live
your loving,
you love your living.*

*Your relationship
with yourself
is also
your relationship
with others.*

*When you are
in the moment,
living happily ever now,
a dream has come true.*

Discernment provides beneficial direction along the way.

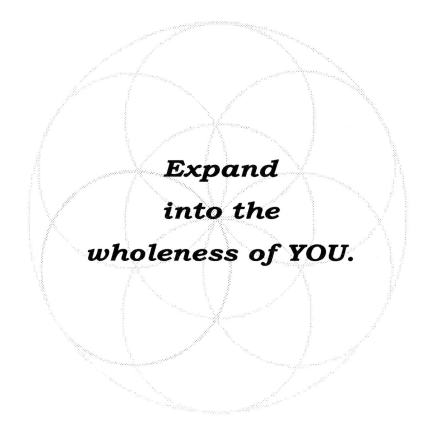

Expand

into the

wholeness of YOU.

*Your unique Self
makes a difference
to the world.*

The journey through life

is a

co-creative process.

When you awaken,

it's good to have

someone close.

The path beyond the

Emerald City

is a Golden Path of LOVE.

*Respectfully
close old doors,
and open new ones
with grace.*

Be aware
that you are leading
with your sole / soul.

Wherever you are,

be present.

*The world awaits
the full expression
of YOU.*

When I experience

your Mastery,

mine awakens.

Live
in the current flow
of your soul.

Discover your true passion.

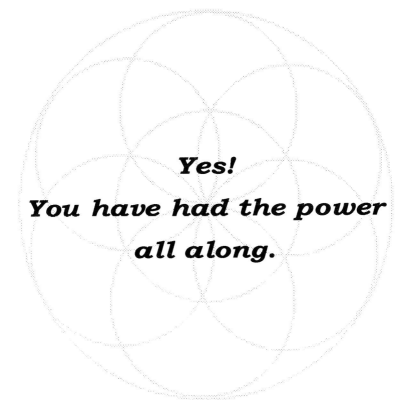

Yes!

You have had the power

all along.

*Wholeness is
where you began.*

*Wholeness is
where you are going.*

*Wholeness is
the All that you are.*

Golden Wizdom Guidelines

Live Knowing Home Lies Within

Love Unconditionally

Be Mindful That Thoughts Create

Trust Your Heart

Courageously Embrace Your Royalty

Celebrate Life

Accept Responsibility for Self-Transformation

Demonstrate the Wisdom and Power of Love

THE EMERALD COUNCIL WITHIN

INTEGRATION OF THE JOURNEY

Our journey has influenced the life of our co-author, Ilene Kimsey. She has used our Oz experience as an archetype for understanding her life in a fuller way. We have been a metaphor for her to embrace aspects of herself. In the process, we became a part of her personal Council. We have asked Ilene to share some of the things she has discovered. We believe you, too, will find them valuable to your life experience.

My Own Journey

Thank you my *Toto*-ly Ozsome friends! What an amazing journey we are experiencing! I am deeply appreciative for how you have expanded my world. I am honored to share my insights with the reader.

I have been consciously interacting with the Oz characters since 1983. My subconscious relationship began when I was Kansas-born into the mystique of *The Wizard of Oz*. To be from Kansas was synonymous with living on a farm, and having Dorothy and Toto for neighbors. I often wished they did live down the road. There was so much I would have liked to talk about with Dorothy.

My intimacy with the pure essence of Oz and the mastery of each character has been my path of passion. I am honored at a soul level to be in such a profound relationship with each of these energies of love. This interactive association has increased my ability to embrace many aspects of my Self. I am honored to share a brief overview of my journey and some practical application tools for daily living that I have learned through this Oz adventure.

A tornado of turmoil entered my life by way of my Mother's death, the discovery of cervical pre-cancer cells, a divorce, and the loss of a job. My theme song that year became, "What's It All About, Alfie?" I felt as if every aspect of my being was frustrated and confused. There was an internal debate taking place. The questions up for scrutiny were: *Who am I? Why am I here? What do I do with all these shattered pieces? How can I trust my heart again? What is my truth? Do I have the courage to make new choices? Where do I begin?*

It was devastating to see my life lying before me in broken fragments. The experience was similar to returning to your home after a tornado, earthquake, hurricane, or other natural disaster. In the aftershock, you begin picking up some of the pieces in an attempt to find something recognizable.

Since my previous paradigm for life had fractured, I needed an archetype, an original pattern or model, as a reference for rebuilding. The story of *The Wizard of Oz* was an easily accessible metaphor to use as my life's new architectural blueprint.

OZ MENTORS

All of me was searching for answers. I was wide open with the desire to know, *Who am I? Why am I here?* In response to these questions, my Oz mentors arose from my creative subconscious to accompany me on my journey to rediscovering my Self. Instead of traveling alone, I had a council of experts at my side.

One by one, I picked up the shattered pieces and began to sort through what I found. Each character guided me, by example, to explore all aspects of my fragmented self. I was grateful for a familiar form in which to process the issues that had backed up like a sewer in my life.

For five years, I carried on a dialogue with each of the Oz characters. I invited them to assist me in the pursuit to make renewed sense out of my life. When an issue came up within me, I would call upon the character that most aligned with that matter of concern. During this life restructuring, I also used tools from my academic background in human development and my professional work in business consulting and family counseling. Blending my professional knowledge of human development with the Oz metaphor created a powerful resource for personal transformation.

COUNCIL: ONE OUT OF MANY

I discovered that each character represented an aspect of myself: Dorothy, the spiritual; Scarecrow, the mental; Tin Woodman, the emotional; and Lion, the physical. This realization awakened me even more to the importance of embracing all parts of me. Throughout my life, I had often made decisions based upon what I *thought* while discounting what I *felt*. Other times, I made choices purely from physical desire, disregarding the wisdom and guidance of the emotional, mental, and spiritual bodies. This method of interaction left me off balance.

I began looking at myself as a *whole body* or *system* rather than a group of disconnected pieces. Initially, this viewpoint was very overwhelming. I had to expand my limited concept of myself. The Oz characters supported me in understanding how unique individuals can work together as One. I used the interrelationship between Dorothy, the Scarecrow, Tin Woodman, and the Lion as a reference for the inner relationship of my spirit, mind, heart, and body.

I made a commitment to create a more functional communication system with my spiritual, mental, emotional, and physical components. I created the image of a big, round table with a large, beautiful emerald gem at the center. The emerald symbolizes my commitment to communicate from the heart. At this Emerald Council table of equality, I listen to the truths offered by all aspects of my Self. The Council provides a forum to recognize the wisdom of spirit, mind, heart, and body.

The Emerald Council has taught me to simultaneously *observe* and *participate* in my life. When making an important decision, I gather input from all aspects of myself. There is a sense of integrity and strength in this experience of Council. The integration of One out of the many is empowering.

When I received the idea to work full time on completing the writing of *Golden Wizdom Beyond The Emerald City*, I used the Council forum to process my many thoughts and feelings. The Council table provided a neutral space to listen to the varied aspects of my inner dialogue. On the following pages is an example of the type of discussions that took place at these Emerald Council meetings.

Topic for Discussion:

Working full time to complete the writing of *Golden Wizdom Beyond The Emerald City.*

Mental Body

Are you crazy? How are we going to take care of ourselves financially if we're not getting paid for what we're doing? This just isn't a logical choice. On the other hand, I know that if we don't give ourselves time and space to accomplish this task, it will never be completed. I need more input to create other options.

Emotional Body

I have a peaceful knowing that now is the time for the full commitment to complete the book. I am thrilled, excited, nervous, and a bit fearful. My strongest awareness is an absolute certainty that NOW is the time for manifesting dreams.

Physical Body

The tension in me melts away when I picture the opportunity to totally focus on writing. If I know our basic needs are taken care of, I can relax. In that comfort, I can allow the creativity to move through me and onto the paper. The bottom line is, I need to know our physical needs are taken care of.

Spiritual Body

This is the time for the completion of this book. I know that all is in place and taken care of. Our part is to connect in wholeness to our common decision. Together we will co-create the reality. We are to have a clear intention, make a full commitment, and take practical action steps. With our pieces in place, the Universe will support the project.

After many such dialogues, all aspects were in agreement to commit our full focus on the completion of the book. Even though the Council meetings are *me* talking to *me*, I say, *our*, to emphasize that I have different dimensions or bodies with unique needs.

The process of integrating what I have gleaned from the metaphor of *The Wizard of Oz* and the Oz characters has been on going for seventeen years. I have come to understand that I was interacting with my Self in a disjointed manner. This incomplete communication was *missed communication,* and resulted in *disunity.* I was only partially involved with the decisions I made. This segregated living was not in my highest interest. I was not experiencing life as fully as I knew I could or that I desired. I chose to *re-form* my life and integrate all parts of me into the *whole body.*

The journey of the Oz seekers continues to be a resource for designing my life. Their unique wizdom provides a powerful format for living with integrity. I have embraced the eight *Golden Wizdom Guidelines* as an inner guidance system for my continued life adventure.

> *Live knowing home lies within*
> *Love unconditionally*
> *Be mindful that thoughts create*
> *Trust your heart*
> *Courageously embrace your royalty*
> *Celebrate life*
> *Accept responsibility for self-transformation*
> *Demonstrate the wisdom and power of Love.*

In the activity section, you will have an opportunity to apply these *Golden Wizdom Guidelines* to your life's design. You will engage with your spiritual, mental, emotional, and physical wisdom and integrate them into your whole body system.

Honor Your Journey

This journey is uniquely yours. You are the leading authority for your life's mastery. Like the century-old Masters of Oz, you know that all you have been looking for lies within. Through participation in life, you have acquired your own wisdom. The life choices you have made, consciously or unconsciously, brought you to this place on your path. Each moment is a new opportunity to choose your next step. It is important to respect where you have been, where you are now, and where you are going. This journey is a dynamic, inner action between the spiritual, mental, emotional, and physical aspects of yourself. When these unique dimensions are in alignment with one another, your whole body system moves in harmony.

The Personal Council and Life Application Activities will help you access this inner knowledge. They will support you in acknowledging your wisdom and embracing your whole Self. The activities provide a format to honor your life's journey, and to respect the choices you have made and will make along the way.

Honor Your Choice

Before you begin these activities, it is important to recognize that each of us has a preferred learning style. Your unique learning style is a combination of the way you take in information and how you access previous experience. You may learn best by utilizing one or more of the following approaches: by *seeing* the information demonstrated; by *hearing* the information; by *writing* about the information; by *talking* about the information; or by *physically experiencing* the information. Each of these approaches allows you to process data in a different way: visually, verbally, or kinesthetically. It is of value to be aware of which approach *looks, sounds,* or *feels* most natural to you.

Depending on your learning preference, you may choose different ways to express the information being explored through the Personal Council and the Life Application Activities. Here are some possible options:

Visual Learner

Use your imagination to create a visual image. Cut out pictures to create a collage, or draw images of your thoughts, feelings, and experiences.

Auditory/ Verbal Learner

Use an audio tape to record your response, or talk about your thoughts, feelings, and experiences with a friend.

Kinesthetic Learner

Use movement in the form of writing, drawing, or some other action oriented expression. Create a notebook or personalize a journal to record your thoughts, feelings, and experiences.

Allow yourself the freedom to creatively interact with these activities in the manner that serves you most effectively.

Personal Council Activity

This activity in an exploration of your mental, emotional, physical, and spiritual response to each *Golden Wizdom Guideline*. Developing an awareness of these aspects creates the foundation for wise inner communication. A healthy relationship with your Self is the doorway to healthy relationships with others. When your system is functioning as one *whole* body, possibilities expand.

This Council gathering is similar to calling together a Board meeting to discuss business. Following are options for setting up your Personal Council meeting.

Invite the members of your Council, your Body, Mind, Heart, and Spirit, to join this important gathering. (Example: *I invite all aspects of my Self, my Body, Mind, Heart, and Spirit to join me in a Council meeting.*)

State the purpose of the meeting. (Example: *The purpose of this meeting is to be aware of my various levels of response to the Golden Wizdom Guidelines.*)

Read the Guidelines and reflect on your response to each statement. Remember, you may choose to visually image, write, draw, or talk about your response.

Allow yourself time for quality interaction with each Guideline. You may choose to focus on one a day, a week, or a month. Trust your inner guidance.

Thank your Personal Council members for their participation in the meeting. (Example: *Dear Body,*

Mind, Heart, and Spirit, I am grateful for your full participation in this Council meeting.) Thank your Self for this inner action. Through this process, you are developing a practical method for listening to and honoring all aspects of your Self.

The following partial statements are offered for your completion:

Live Knowing Home Lies Within
    As I reflect on this statement:
    I think . . .
    I feel . . .
    I physically experience...
    I know . . .
    It is my intention to . . .

Love Unconditionally
    As I reflect on this statement:
    I think . . .
    I feel . . .
    I physically experience . . .
    I know . . .
    It is my intention to . . .

Be Mindful That Thoughts Create
    As I reflect on this statement:
    I think . . .
    I feel . . .
    I physically experience . . .
    I know . . .
    It is my intention to . . .

Trust Your Heart
As I reflect on this statement:
I think . . .
I feel . . .
I physically experience . . .
I know . . .
It is my intention to . . .

Courageously Embrace Your Royalty
As I reflect on this statement:
I think . . .
I feel . . .
I physically experience . . .
I know . . .
It is my intention to . . .

Celebrate Life
As I reflect on this statement:
I think . . .
I feel . . .
I physically experience . . .
I know . . .
It is my intention to . . .

Accept Responsibility for Self-Transformation
As I reflect on this statement:
I think . . .
I feel . . .
I physically experience . . .
I know . . .
It is my intention to . . .

Demonstrate the Wisdom and Power of Love
    As I reflect on this statement:
    I think . . .
    I feel . . .
    I physically experience . . .
    I know . . .
    It is my intention to . . .

Life Application Activity

This activity is about consciously designing your life to reflect your wholeness. It is an opportunity to *review* your life's journey, *renew* your choices, and *consciously be and do* what you intend. Through the process of *integration, appreciation,* and *celebration,* you will put your intentions into motion.

Create a quiet time and space to do this activity. You may choose to complete the process in one session, or take a week or more to explore a topic. Honor your intuition, listen to your inner voice, and trust your gut feeling. Respect all aspects of yourself and allow the time you need to assimilate what you discover. The activity is a tool. You are the master craftsman. This is *your* journey. Proceed in a way that serves you.

Gather your Personal Council:

Call your Council to support you in this process.

Select one of the following options for further exploration:

Oz character anecdote from "The Journey."

Anecdote refers to an entertaining account of a real or fictitious occurrence.

Choose a character anecdote that has special interest for you and investigate insights you have gained.

Past experience from your life.

Reflect on a life experience that you would like to have some completion with, or understand more deeply.

Present challenge you are having in your life.

Transform a daily challenge into a valued opportunity.

Review

Write down the topic or subject you have chosen for this Life Application Activity. (Example: *My move from Hawaii to Colorado.*)
What are some of the highlights?

What are the facts, feelings, or images of this experience that have special significance?

Renew

Respond to any or all of the following statements that will help you explore what you discovered in the *Review*:
The clarity I have now is . . .

Something I am ready to get closure on, is . . .

An old habit, attitude, or belief I am ready to change is . . .

A judgment I am ready to release is . . .
Something I would like to heal, or someone I would like to forgive is . . .

My teacher in this situation is . . .

A new way I can look at this experience is . . .

One of the gifts of this experience is . . .

Some wisdom I have gained is . . .

Consciously Be and Do

Allow yourself to go to your *home* within. In that place of sanctuary and inner knowing, confirm your personal insights and the wisdom you gained. Create a conscious intent for action.
What do I choose to *be* now? (Example: *I choose to be in a state of clarity and peace as I make decisions about moving.*)

What do I choose to *do* now? (Example: *I choose to gracefully and lovingly say "Aloha" to Hawaii and take practical steps to plan my move to Colorado.*)

Integration

Webster's Dictionary defines *integrate*: To make or become whole or complete; to bring parts together into a whole. This integration process supports you in aligning what you *consciously* choose to *be* and *do* into each aspect of yourself. When all of our aspects, body, mind, heart, and spirit, are going in the same direction, there can be grace and ease in forward movement.

Heart (Emotional Body) - Integrate your choice into your emotional body. As you inhale slowly, think about your choice. On your exhale, breathe the power of Love into your choice. With each beat of your heart, feel the pulse of life activating your choice. Experience the emotions (energy in motion) of joy, peace, satisfaction, etc., associated with your choice.

Mind (Mental Body) - Use the gift of your mental body to create an image of accomplishing your choice. In your creatively conscious mind, when describing your experience, use the first person, present tense. (Example: *I am grateful for a smooth transition. I am enjoying my new home in Colorado. I am delighting in the fresh mountain air.*)

Body (Physical Body) - Engage your entire body in experiencing your choice. Allow your thoughts and feelings to be felt in every cell of your being, from the top of your head to the soles of your feet. Take physical action with your choice. (Example: *I am enjoying the celebration party to say good-bye to Hawaii. I feel invigorated as I confirm my Colorado airline reservation.*)

Spirit (Spiritual Body) - The spiritual body holds the pure essence of who you are. As you slowly inhale, carry your choice to the core place within where you interact with Spirit. As you exhale,

release your choice to the vast place beyond you,
where the infinity of Spirit moves. Know that you
and your choice are held in the wisdom and
power of pure Love.

Appreciation

Give thanks to your Self and all aspects of yourself,
body, mind, heart, and spirit. Acknowledge all those
who have been teachers along the way in assisting
you in being who you are in this moment.

You may choose to write a thank you note, meditate, or
say a prayer of thanksgiving. Expressing gratitude
integrates the reality of your new choices more
deeply.

Celebration

Celebrate your conscious choice to live in a new state of
awareness. Choose a manner of celebration that
means something special to you. Your expression of
delight may be through speaking, writing, singing,
drawing, or moving.

Proclaim your delight by simply saying, "Yes," or "Way
to go!" You could light a candle, take a bath, dance,
have a nice meal. Whatever expression you choose,
remember to invite your whole being to the
celebration.

Beyond the Re-union

Welcome Home! This journey to the heart has brought us back to ourselves. Like the Oz characters, we have discovered that all we were looking for lies within. Being in the Oz experience is being in the state of wholeness. From that dynamic reference, our thoughts create the moment, our heart's desire is realized, and our royalty is recognized.

Golden Wizdom Beyond The Emerald City is a conscious journey to wholeness, a pilgrimage home to inner wisdom. Awareness creates a world of new choices. It has been my intent to provide opportunities for you to awaken to life in a renewed way. When we consciously co-create life's journey, our options multiply. The tornadoes in our life can become a gift of spiraling energy carrying us to a new perspective. The fears can be invitations to release that which serves us no longer. Expanding the awareness of the wisdom of our body, mind, heart, and spirit gives wise counsel to our personal authority.

What the Oz characters stated about themselves at the beginning of our journey can now be spoken by you and me.

Each of us is a Master in our own right. We are ready to be seen as who we really are, not who we were. It is time to embrace our knowing and our mastery.

Receive the wholeness of who you are and the insights of your own Golden Wizdom. May you continue to explore the magnitude of your *ozsomeness*.

As you journey, so do we.
As we journey, so do you
Together we are One.

We are - ONLY LOVE.

EMERALD GEMS

I am the wisdom of light
that lies within the innocence of you.

I am the wisdom of unconditional love
that lies within the essence of your being.

I am the wisdom of creation
that lies within the thought of you.

I am the wisdom of truth
that lies within the heart of you.

I am the wisdom of royalty
that lies within each cell of your body.

I am the magic of joy
woven within each breath you take.

I am the magic of transformation
dancing through your being.

I am the wisdom of power
that lies within the core of your love.

We are the Oneness
that lies within the many aspects of you.

Masters of Oz

Photo by Katie Carroll

Ilene Kimsey is a creative life educator who delights in setting a stage for people to experience their greatness. She has a master's degree in Human Development from Pacific Oaks College in Pasadena, California. Ilene has a refined understanding of the Oz metaphor as a tool for transformation which she has developed over nearly two decades. She has worked professionally for thirty years, serving as a business training coordinator, education consultant, and attitudinal healing counselor. She is a speaker, an experiential seminar presenter, a songwriter, and the author of a self-esteem program for children,. Ilene was born and grew up in Manhattan, Kansas. Over the years, she has made her home in the heartland of Iowa and Minnesota, the creative spirit of Southern California, and the culturally rich diversity of Hawaii. Presently Ilene lives in Loveland, Colorado.

Nan No'eau Penner. A lifetime of creating and teaching art has taken No'eau to California, Washington, Alaska, New Mexico, Washington, D.C., Hawaii, and Japan to share her delight in weaving, paper making, painting, and sculpture. She honors her ancestors and teachers, and passes the teaching wand on to her three children, Kym, Tod, and Dea. No'eau brings light and love into this universe by making art, teaching art and celebrating the very precious nature of life with her husband Ralph in the mountains of Northern California.

Photo by Ralph Penner

To arrange a speaking engagement or experiential seminar, please send your requests to the following mailing or e-mail address. Also, your comments on the ideas presented in this book are welcome.

Ilene Kimsey
Toto-ly Ozsome Publishing
P.O. Box 96
Loveland, Co 80539
E-mail: golden_wizdom@yahoo.com